Lord Neaves

Songs and Verses Social and Scientific

Lord Neaves

Songs and Verses Social and Scientific

ISBN/EAN: 9783337007089

Printed in Europe, USA, Canada, Australia, Japan

Cover: Foto ©Thomas Meinert / pixelio.de

More available books at **www.hansebooks.com**

SONGS AND VERSES.

Extracts from Reviews.

SATURDAY REVIEW.

"The productions thrown off by this eccentric muse have all the merits of originality and variety. . . . He has written songs, not essays—such a hotch-potch of science and humour, jest and literature, gossip and criticism, as might have been served at the Noctes Ambrosianæ in the blue parlour at Ambrose's."

NOTES AND QUERIES.

"The songs are rich in humour; they are pervaded by a genial view of human life, and they are an admirable mixture of wit and wisdom."

SCOTSMAN.

"And even without the pleasing accessories of such an occasion, without the good company and all the softening influences that come 'with the walnuts and the wine'—in the cold daylight of print, the abounding and concentrated humour of these sunny social lyrics tickles the reader to repeated smiles, if not to continuous or audible laughter. . . . Graceful lively trifles convivial even to hilarity, but still always decorous, and keeping within the limits of becoming mirth."

GLASGOW HERALD.

"If the general reader still retains the capacity for being amused, if he is willing to descend from the heights of solemn discussion and argument to kindly humour, not without a flavour of genial scholarship, then he will welcome this literary visit from an Old Contributor to 'Maga.'"

SONGS AND VERSES

SOCIAL AND SCIENTIFIC

SONGS AND VERSES

SOCIAL AND SCIENTIFIC

BY

AN OLD CONTRIBUTOR TO *MAGA*

THIRD EDITION, ENLARGED

WITH

THE MUSIC OF SOME OF THE SONGS

WILLIAM BLACKWOOD AND SONS
EDINBURGH AND LONDON
MDCCCLXIX

PREFACE.

A GREAT proportion of these pieces were originally published in 'Blackwood's Magazine;' some appeared in the 'Scotsman' Newspaper; and the rest were written for the amusement of a Scientific Club, or of a circle of private friends. They were received at the time with some approbation; and they are now collected mainly in the hope of preserving or reviving in the minds of those who were then pleased to approve of them a recollection of the feelings that attended their first reception.

CONTENTS.

	PAGE
THE ORIGIN OF SPECIES	1
THE MEMORY OF MONBODDO	6
THE DARWINIAN ERA OF FARMING	9
THE ORIGIN OF LANGUAGE	12
GRIMM'S LAW	16
STUART MILL ON MIND AND MATTER	21
A FLASK OF ROSY WINE	26
I'M VERY FOND OF WATER	30
THE PERMISSIVE BILL	33
HALF-SEAS OVER	36
A BOTTLE AND FRIEND	39
THE PLANTING OF THE VINE	41
GASTER, THE FIRST M.A.	44
GASTER (A LYRICAL VERSION)	49
BEEF AND POTATOES	53
A SONG OF PROVERBS	56
A SONG OF TRUISMS	60

SONG AT THE SYMPOSIUM ON MAGA	63
HILLI-ONNEE	68
THE THREE R'S	71
O WHY SHOULD A WOMAN NOT GET A DEGREE?	74
THE READING OF GREEK	77
HOW TO MAKE A NOVEL	81
AD SODALITATIS HELLENICÆ SOCIOS	85
THE PROPOSAL OF POLTYS	88
THE PENNY OF PASES	91
LET US ALL BE UNHAPPY ON SUNDAY	95
THE THREE MODERATORS	98
THE TOURIST'S MATRIMONIAL GUIDE THROUGH SCOTLAND	101
DECIMIS INCLUSIS	105
SATURDAY AT E'EN	108
O! HE WAS LANG O' COMING	111
THE JOLLY TESTATOR WHO MAKES HIS OWN WILL	115
HEY FOR SOCIAL SCIENCE, O!	118
THE SHERIFF'S LIFE AT SEA	123
L'ENVOY	127
MUSIC OF SOME OF THE SONGS	129

SONGS AND VERSES,

SOCIAL AND SCIENTIFIC.

——o——

THE ORIGIN OF SPECIES.

A NEW SONG.

Have you heard of this question the Doctors among,
Whether all living things from a Monad have sprung?
This has lately been said, and it now shall be sung,
      Which nobody can deny.

Not one or two ages sufficed for the feat,
It required a few millions the change to complete;
But now the thing's done, and it looks rather neat,
      Which nobody can deny.

The original Monad, our great-great-grandsire,
To little or nothing at first did aspire;
But at last to have offspring it took a desire,
    Which nobody can deny.

This Monad becoming a father or mother,
By budding or bursting, produced such another;
And shortly there followed a sister or brother,
    Which nobody can deny.

But Monad no longer designates them well—
They're a cluster of molecules now, or a cell;
But which of the two, Doctors only can tell,
    Which nobody can deny.

These beings, increasing, grew buoyant with life,
And each to itself was both husband and wife;
And at first, strange to say, the two lived without strife,
    Which nobody can deny.

But such crowding together soon troublesome grew,
And they thought a division of labour would do;
So their sexual system was parted in two,
    Which nobody can deny.

Thus Plato supposes that, severed by fate,
Human halves run about, each in search of its mate,
Never pleased till they gain their original state,
        Which nobody can deny.

Excrescences fast were now trying to shoot;
Some put out a finger, some put out a foot;
Some set up a mouth, and some sent down a root,
        Which nobody can deny.

Some, wishing to walk, manufactured a limb;
Some rigged out a fin, with a purpose to swim;
Some opened an eye, some remained dark and dim,
        Which nobody can deny.

Some creatures grew bulky, while others were small,
As nature sent food for the few or for all;
And the weakest, we know, ever go to the wall,
        Which nobody can deny.

A deer with a neck that was longer by half
Than the rest of its family's (try not to laugh),
By stretching and stretching, became a Giraffe,
        Which nobody can deny.

A very tall pig, with a very long nose,
Sends forth a proboscis quite down to his toes;
And he then by the name of an Elephant goes,
        Which nobody can deny.

The four-footed beast that we now call a Whale,
Held its hind-legs so close that they grew to a tail,
Which it uses for threshing the sea like a flail,
        Which nobody can deny.

Pouters, tumblers, and fantails are from the same source;
The racer and hack may be traced to one Horse:
So Men were developed from Monkeys, of course,
        Which nobody can deny.

An Ape with a pliable thumb and big brain,
When the gift of the gab he had managed to gain,
As a Lord of Creation established his reign,
        Which nobody can deny.

But I'm sadly afraid, if we do not take care,
A relapse to low life may our prospects impair;
So of beastly propensities let us beware,
        Which nobody can deny.

Their lofty position our children may lose,
And, reduced to all-fours, must then narrow their views;
Which would wholly unfit them for filling our shoes,
        Which nobody can deny.

Their vertebræ next might be taken away,
When they'd sink to an oyster, or insect, some day,
Or the pitiful part of a polypus play,
        Which nobody can deny.

Thus losing Humanity's nature and name,
And descending through varying stages of shame,
They'd return to the Monad, from which we all came,
        Which nobody can deny.

May 1861.

THE MEMORY OF MONBODDO.

AN EXCELLENT NEW SONG.

AIR—*The Looking-Glass.*

'TIS strange how men and things revive
    Though laid beneath the sod, O!
I sometimes think I see alive
    Our good old friend Monboddo!
His views, when forth at first they came,
    Appeared a little odd, O!
But now we've notions much the same;
    We're back to old Monboddo.

The rise of Man he loved to trace
    Up to the very pod, O!
And in Baboons our parent race
    Was found by old Monboddo.
Their A B C he made them speak,
    And learn their *Qui, quæ, quod*, O!
Till Hebrew, Latin, Welsh, and Greek
    They knew as well's Monboddo.

The Memory of Monboddo.

The thought that Men had once had tails
   Caused many a grin full broad, O!
And why in us that feature fails,
   Was asked of old Monboddo.
He showed that sitting on the rump,
   While at our work we plod, O!
Would wear th' appendage to the stump
   As close as in Monboddo.

Alas! the good lord little knew,
   As this strange ground he trod, O!
That others would his path pursue,
   And never name Monboddo!
Such folks should have their tails restored,
   And thereon feel the rod, O!
For having thus the fame ignored
   That's due to old Monboddo.

Though Darwin now proclaim the law,
   And spread it far abroad, O!
The man that first the secret saw,
   Was honest old Monboddo.
The Architect precedence takes
   Of him that bears the hod, O!
So up and at them, Land of Cakes!
   We'll vindicate Monboddo.

The Scotchman who would grudge his praise,
    Must be a senseless clod, O !
A MONUMENT then let us raise,
    To honour old Monboddo.
Let some great artist sketch the plan,
    While Rogers* gives the nod, O !
A Monkey changing to a Man !
    In memory of Monboddo.

* The Rev. promoter of the Wallace Monument.

September 1861.

THE DARWINIAN ERA OF FARMING.

Air—*Derry Down*.

O! FARMING'S not merely an art of some skill;
It's a Science, or something more excellent still:
For the Farmer has such a command over nature,
You almost might call him a kind of Creator:

Singing down, down, down, derry down.

'Twas long ago found that a Horse and an Ass
Breed a good kind of beast for a mountainous pass;
But since Mules were invented, it never till now
Was supposed you could breed from a Horse and a Cow:

Singing down, down, down, derry down.

But all nowadays to their lessons must look:
So the Farmer must read Mr Darwin's great book,
Who proves or asserts, and has credit from some,
That from all sorts of creatures all others may come:

Singing down, down, down, derry down.

If this theory holds, and we find the right way,
There's no end of the freaks that the Farmer may play;
Getting all sorts of products from all sorts of stocks,
He may ride on his Ram and clip wool from his Ox :

    Singing down, down, down, derry down.

He may breed you a beast mingled just half and half,
From a fortunate cross of a Pig and a Calf;
When you'll cut without trouble, so neat and so nice,
Both your ham and your veal in the very same slice :

    Singing down, down, down, derry down.

As now well established beyond any question,
Variety's good both for taste and digestion;
And a Hybrid would prove a prodigious relief,
With the fore-quarter *mutton*, the hind-quarter *beef* :

    Singing down, down, down, derry down.

You must never lose heart if your mules seldom breed,
Or if some of your mixtures at first don't succeed ;
Mr Darwin himself would exhort you to wait,
As he draws his own bills at a very long date :

    Singing down, down, down, derry down.

So, perhaps, when their practical worth you explore,
There's not much in these notions we hadn't before;
For they'll scarcely come true (what a subject for laughter!)
Till the great day of Judgment,—or say the day After:

Singing down, down, down, derry down.

THE ORIGIN OF LANGUAGE.

AN EXCELLENT NEW SONG.

AIR—*Let Schoolmasters puzzle their brains.*

'TIS not very easy to say
   How language had first a beginning,
When Adam had just left the clay,
   And Eve hadn't taken to spinning;
Or if we suppose them to spring
   Tongue-tied from the lower creation,
What power cut their chattering string,
   Or prompted their speechification?
     Toroddle, toroddle, toroll.

Some think men were ready inspired
   With lexicon, syntax, and grammar,
And never like children required
   At lessons to lisp and to stammer.
As Pallas by Jove was begot
   In armour all brilliantly burnished,

The Origin of Language.

So Man with his Liddell and Scott
   And old Lindley Murray was furnished.
     Toroddle, toroddle, toroll.

Some say that the primitive tongue
   Expressed but the simplest affections;
And swear that the words said or sung
   Were nothing but mere Interjections.
O! O! was the signal of pain:
   Ha! Ha! was the symptom of laughter:
Pooh! Pooh! was the sign of disdain,
   And *Hillo!* came following after.
     Toroddle, toroddle, toroll.

Some, taking a different view,
   Maintain the old language was fitted
To mark out the objects we knew,
   By mimicking sounds they emitted.
Bow, wow was the name for a dog:
   Quack, quack was the word for a duckling:
Hunc, hunc would designate a hog,
   And *wee, wee* a pig and a suckling.
     Toroddle, toroddle, toroll.

Who knows if what Adam might speak,
   Was mono- or poly-syllabic;

Was Gothic, or Gaelic, or Greek,
    Tartaric, Chinese, or Arabic.
It may have been Sanscrit or Zend–
    It must have been something or other;
But thus far I'll stoutly contend,
    It wasn't the tongue of his mother.

    Toroddle, toroddle, toroll.

If asked these hard things to explain,
    I own I am wholly unable;
And hold the attempt the more vain,
    When I think of the building of Babel.
Then why should we puzzle our brains
    With Etymological clatter?
The prize wouldn't prove worth the pains,
    And the missing it isn't much matter.

    Toroddle, toroddle, toroll.

In courtship suppose you can't sing,
    Your Cara, your Liebe, your Zoe,
A kiss and a sight of the ring
    Will more quickly prevail with your Chloe.
Or if you in twenty strange tongues
    Could call for a beef-steak and bottle,

A purse with less learning and lungs,
   Would bring them much nearer your throttle.
      Toroddle, toroddle, toroll.

I've ranged, without drinking a drop,
   The realms of the dry Mithridates:
I've studied Grimm, Burnouf, and Bopp,
   Till patience cried " *Ohe jam satis.*"
Max Müller completed my plan,
   And, leave of the subject now taking,
As wise as when first I began,
   I end with a head that is aching.
      Toroddle, toroddle, toroll.

The speech of Old England for me;
   It serves us on every occasion!
Henceforth, like our soil, let it be
   Exempted from foreign invasion.
It answers for friendship and love,
   For all sorts of feeling and thinking;
And lastly, all doubt to remove—
   It answers for singing and drinking.
      Toroddle, toroddle, toroll.

February 1862.

GRIMM'S LAW.

[*In a late Number of the 'Anthropological Review' Grimm's law is explained in what is at least an ingenious manner. After describing an Aryan, or "articulate-speaking man," setting out to teach language to some rude owners of the "kitchen-middens" of the primeval age, who are supposed to be speechless, a distinguished Anthropologist thus reports the result of the attempt:* "*But now assume the* 200 [*kitchen-middeners*] *to be mutes, and follow the leader of the Aryans in his first lesson to the crowd around him. Naturally he would get the crowd to pronounce after him some short syllables, such as* pa, ta, ka, *to illustrate the use of lips, palate, and throat, and very naturally the four or five men* (*or women more likely*) *just in front of him would pronounce them rightly, but not one man in fifty can tell the real effect of his work on a crowd. On their returning to their wigwams, much would be the emotion of risibility and imitativeness displayed that night among the natives; and next morning the chances are that the majority who stood some distance from the speaker would have fixed for ever upon the whole nation the wrong utterance of* ba, da, ga. *The main point of my whole argument is, that such a result would most naturally follow among mutes, but would never happen among speaking men.*"—Extract from Paper read before the Anthropological Society by the Rev. D. I. HEATH, M.A.—'Anthropological Review,' April 1867.]

GRIMM'S LAW.

A NEW SONG.

A<small>IR</small>—*Old Homer,—but with him what have we to do?*

ETYMOLOGY once was a wild kind of thing,
 Which from any one word any other could bring:
Of the consonants then the effect was thought small,
And the vowels—the vowels were nothing at all.
   Down a down, down, &c.

But that state of matters completely is changed,
And the old school of scholars now feels quite estranged:
For 'tis clear that whenever we open our jaw,
Every sound that we utter comes under some Law.

Now one of these laws has been named after Grimm,
For the Germans declare it was found out by him:
But their rivals the Danes take the Germans to task,
And proclaim as its finder the great Rasmus Rask.

Be this as it may, few have sought to explain
How it came that this law could its influence gain:
Max Müller has tried, and, perhaps, pretty well;
But I don't understand him, and therefore can't tell.

Anthropologists say, after Man had his birth,
There were two human races possessing the earth;
One gifted and graced with articulate speech,
And another that only could gabble and screech.

The Aryans could speak, and could build, and could plough,
And knew most of the arts we are practising now;
But the Dumbies that dwelt at those vile Kitchen-Middens
Weren't fit but to do their superiors' biddings.

So an Aryan went forth to enlighten these others,
And to raise them by speech to the level of brothers;
On the Mutes of the Middens he burst with éclat,
And attempted to teach them the syllable PA.

This PA was intended to set things a-going
For a lot of Good Words very well worth the knowing;
Such as Pater, and πολις, and Panis, and Pasco;
But the Midden performers made rather a *fiasco*.

Scarce one of them all would say PA for a wonder,
But each blundered away with a different blunder:
Some feebly cried A, and some, crow-like, said KA,
While the nearest they came to was FA or was BA.

Then the Aryan propounded the syllable TA,
Which his pupils corrupted to THA and to DA :
Even KA, when they tried it, they never came nearer
Than to HA or to GA, or to something still queerer.

So slow were their senses to seize what was said,
That they never could hit the right nail on the head ;
And the game of cross purposes lasted so long,
That it soon was a rule they should always go wrong.

Thus the Dumbies for ever said Father for Pater,
And Bearing and Brother for Ferens and Frater :
The Aryan cried Pecu, the Midden-man Fee,
In which Doctors and Lawyers to this day agree.

Jove's Tonitru sank into Old Saxon Thunner,
Which the High-German dunderheads changed into Donner ;
From Domo came Tame, and from Domus came Timmer,
While the hissing Helvetians said Zämen and Zimmer.

From θυρα came Door, and from θυγατηρ Dochter,
Which dwindled away into Türe and Tochter ;
From Hortus and Hostis came Garden and Guest,
And from χολη came Gall, which so bothers the best.

The Old Aryan G<small>AU</small> was the Kitchener's K<small>OO</small>
(Though some tribes were contented to call the beast
    Boo):
If your wife in her καρδια would give you a Cornu,
The Midden-man said, " In her Heart she would Horn
    you."

Such a roundabout race I can only compare
To the whirligig engines we mount at a fair;
Where each rides as in fear lest his steed be forsaken,
But he ne'er overtakes, and is ne'er overtaken.

A theory seldom is free from a flaw,
But the story I've told may account for Grimm's law:
Though some others suggest, if the Bible's no fable,
That Grimm's law was what caused the confusion at
    Babel.
        Down a down, down, &c.

December 1867.

STUART MILL ON MIND AND MATTER.*

A NEW SONG.

AIR—*Roy's Wife of Aldivalloch.*

Stuart Mill, on Mind and Matter,
All our old Beliefs would scatter:
   Stuart Mill exerts his skill
To make an end of Mind and Matter.

THE self-same tale I've surely heard,
   Employed before, our faith to batter:
Has David Hume again appeared,
   To run a-muck at Mind and Matter?

---

* "Matter, then, may be defined a Permanent Possibility of Sensation."
—*Mill's Examination of Hamilton*, p. 198.

"The belief I entertain that my mind exists, when it is not feeling, nor thinking, nor conscious of its own existence, resolves itself into the belief of a Permanent Possibility of these states." "The Permanent Possibility of feeling, which forms my notion of Myself."—*Ibid.*, p. 205, 206.

*David Hume could Mind and Matter
Ruthlessly assault and batter:
　Those who Hume would now exhume
　Must mean to end both Mind and Matter.*

Now Mind, now Matter, to destroy,
　Was oft proposed, at least the latter:
But David was the daring boy
　Who fairly floored *both* Mind and Matter.

*David Hume, both Mind and Matter,
While he lived, would boldly batter:
　Hume by Will bequeathed to Mill
　His favourite feud with Mind and Matter.*

We think we see the Things that be;
　But Truth is coy, we can't get at her;
For what we spy is all my eye,
　And isn't really Mind or Matter.

*Hume and Mill on Mind and Matter
Swear that others merely smatter:
　Sense reveals that Something feels,
　But tells no tale of Mind or Matter.*

Against a stone you strike your toe;
    You feel 'tis sore, it makes a clatter:
But what you feel is all you know
    Of toe, or stone, or Mind, or Matter.

    Mill and Hume of Mind and Matter
    Wouldn't leave a rag or tatter:
        What although we feel the blow?
    That doesn't show there's Mind or Matter.

We meet and mix with other men;
    With women, too, who sweetly chatter:
But mayn't we here be duped again,
    And take our thoughts for Mind and Matter?

    Sights and sounds like Mind and Matter,
    Fairy forms that seem to chatter,
        Are but gleams in Fancy's dreams
    Of Men and Women, Mind and Matter.

Successive feelings on us seize
    (As thick as falling hail-stones patter):
The Chance of some return of these,
    Is all we mean by Mind or Matter.

*Those who talk of Mind and Matter
Just a senseless jargon patter:
  What are We, or you, or he?—
Dissolving views, not Mind or Matter.*

We're but a train of visions vain,
  Of thoughts that cheat, and hopes that flatter:
This hour's our own, the past is flown;
  The rest unknown, like Mind and Matter.

*Then farewell to Mind and Matter:
To the winds at once we scatter
  Time and Place, and Form and Space,
And Heaven and Earth, and Mind and Matter.*

We banish hence Reid's Common Sense;
  We laugh at Dugald Stewart's blatter;
Sir William, too, and Mansel's crew,
  We've done for you, and Mind and Matter.

*Speak no more of Mind and Matter:
Mill with mud may else bespatter
  All your schools of silly fools,
That dare believe in Mind or Matter.*

But had I skill, like Stuart Mill,
   His own position I could shatter:
The weight of Mill, I count as Nil—
   If Mill has neither Mind nor Matter.

Mill, when minus Mind and Matter,
   Though he make a kind of clatter,
     Must himself just mount the shelf,
   And there be laid with Mind and Matter.

I'd push my logic further still
   (Though this may have the look of satire):
I'd prove there's no such man as Mill,—
   If Mill disproves both Mind and Matter.

If there's neither Mind nor Matter,
   Mill's existence, too, we shatter:
     If you still believe in Mill,
   ' *Believe as well in Mind and Matter.*

February 1866.

A FLASK OF ROSY WINE.

A SEMI-SCIENTIFIC SONG.

To make life's pulses gaily go,
    Not much too fast, nor yet too slow;
And joy without dejection know,
    Were worth a golden mine.
Then try with me the simple art,—
If better views you can't impart,—
To calm the brain and cheer the heart
    With a flask of rosy Wine.

Cognac may better suit with some,
Or Gin and Whisky handier come;
And Glasgow long was fond of Rum
    When merchants met to dine:
But Prudence there her part should play,
The fire with water to allay;
Or take instead, to wet her clay,
    A flask of rosy Wine.

The rustic loves a rousing bout
With home-brewed Ale or bottled Stout:
When these are in the sense is out,
    And wit shows little sign.
For dull and dense *his* thoughts appear
That's drinking and that's thinking beer:
There's nothing keeps the head so clear
    As a flask of rosy Wine.

The Poppy's gifts can pain control,
And waft on wings the ravished soul,
While dreamy visions round us roll,
    Where rainbow-hues combine:
But sad reaction comes at last,
And binds the helpless victim fast:
Such gloomy shadows ne'er o'ercast
    The reign of rosy Wine.

The Hemp,—with which we used to hang
Our prison pets, yon felon gang,—
In Eastern climes produces Bang,
    Esteemed a drug divine.
As Hashish dressed, its magic powers
Can lap us in Elysian bowers;
But sweeter far our social hours
    O'er a flask of rosy Wine.

The Tartar's steeds, alive or dead,
Their master keep refreshed and fed;
The steaks they yield, like saddles spread,
    Are cooked beneath his spine:
The milky mothers of his stud,
Outdoing those that chew the cud,
With Koumiss stir his stagnant blood,
    As if with rosy Wine.

The Indian race of famed Peru,
To mash their malt the Chica chew;
And Tonga's tribes the same way brew
    · What serves their Royal line.
The Court collects at dawn of day,
And munching sits and spits away:
The Monarch drinks; but, sooth to say,
    It is not rosy Wine!

A Fungus, on Siberia's plain,
The toper's zeal can so sustain,
That he passes the bottle again and again,
    And gets drunk on the filtered brine.
Our liquor is not quite so strong,
And won't so well the war prolong;
But much the fitter theme for song
    Is our flask of rosy Wine.

Folks up and down will preaching run
That Man should all such influence shun:
They might as well forbid the Sun
    In heaven at noon to shine.
We needs must seek, while here below,
Some kind Nepenthé for our woe;
And what can softer balm bestow
    Than a flask of rosy Wine?

The banquet is not spread in vain,
Nor instincts given to cause us pain;
Though Reason's hand should hold the rein,
    And taste our joys refine:
And trust me, friends, for temperate use
Those vine-clad hills their sweets produce,
And Nature's self exalts the juice
    That fills our flask with Wine.

I'M VERY FOND OF WATER.

A NEW TEMPERANCE SONG.

[Adapted from the Platt Deutsch.]

Ἄριστον μὲν ὕδωρ.

I'M very fond of water,
    I drink it noon and night:
Not Rechab's son or daughter
    Had therein more delight.

I breakfast on it daily;
    And nectar it doth seem,
When once I've mixed it gaily
    With sugar and with cream.
But I forgot to mention
    That in it first I see,
Infused or in suspension,
    Good Mocha or Bohea.

I'm very fond of Water.

CHORUS—*I'm very fond of water,*
  I drink it noon and night:
 No mother's son or daughter
  Hath therein more delight.

At luncheon, too, I drink it,
 And strength it seems to bring:
When really good, I think it
 A liquor for a king.
But I forgot to mention—
 'Tis best to be sincere—
I use an old invention
 That makes it into Beer.

  CHORUS—*I'm very fond of water,* &c.

I drink it, too, at dinner;
 I quaff it full and free,
And find, as I'm a sinner,
 It does not disagree.
But I forgot to mention—
 As thus I drink and dine,
To obviate distension,
 I join some Sherry wine.

  CHORUS—*I'm very fond of water,* &c.

And then when dinner's over,
 And business far away,
I feel myself in clover,
 And sip my *eau sucrée*.
But I forgot to mention—
 To give the glass a smack,
I add, with due attention,
 Glenlivet or Cognac.

  CHORUS—*I'm very fond of water*, &c.

At last when evening closes,
 With something nice to eat,
The best of sleeping doses
 In water still I meet.
But I forgot to mention—
 I think it not a sin
To cheer the day's declension,
 By pouring in some Gin.

CHORUS—*I'm very fond of water:*
 It ever must delight
 Each mother's son or daughter—
 When qualified aright.

June 1861.

THE PERMISSIVE BILL.

A NEW SONG.

"PRAY, what is this Permissive Bill,
 That some folks rave about?
I can't, with all my pains and skill,
 Its meaning quite make out."
O! it's a little simple Bill,
 That seeks to pass *incog.*,
To *permit* ME—to *prevent* YOU—
 From having a glass of grog.
   Yes! it's a little simple Bill, &c.

If I'm a Quaker sly and dry,
 Or Presbyterian sour;
And look on all, with jaundiced eye,
 Who love a joyous hour:
O! here I've my Permissive Bill,
 You naughty boys to flog,
And *permit* ME—to *prevent* YOU—
 From having a glass of grog.
   O! yes, I have my little Bill, &c.

If I have wealth or means enough
    To import a pipe of wine;
While You a glass of humbler stuff
    Must purchase when you dine:
O! then I use my little Bill,
    While wetting well my prog,
To *permit* ME—to *prevent* YOU—
    From buying a glass of grog.

    O! yes, I use my little Bill, &c.

If I'm a fogie quite used up,
    And laid upon the shelf;
Who grudge that You still dine and sup,
    As I was wont myself:
Then I bring out my pretty Bill,
    To impose a little clog,
And *permit* ME—to *prevent* YOU—
    From having a glass of grog.

    Yes, I bring out my pretty Bill, &c.

If You can drink a sober drop,
    While I the bottle drain;
And as I don't know when to stop,
    I'm ordered to "abstain:"

The Permissive Bill.

O! then I've my Permissive Bill,
    Since I'm a drunken dog,
To *permit* ME—to *prevent* YOU—
    Enjoying a glass of grog.

    O! yes, I've my Permissive Bill, &c.

" However well a man behaves,
    Life's pleasures must he lose,
Because a lot of fools or knaves
    Dislike them, or abuse?"
O! yes, and soon a bigger Bill,
    Will go the total hog,
And *permit* ME—to *prevent* YOU—
    Having Mirth as well as Grog.

    CHORUS—*O! yes, a big Permissive Bill,*
        Will go the Total Hog,
        And permit ME—*to* prevent YOU—
        Having Liberty, Mirth, or Grog.

June 1866.

HALF-SEAS OVER.

A BACCHANALIAN SONG.

"*Entre deux vins.*"

Air—*Cauld Kail.*

SOME jolly dogs are drunk outright
    From All-Saints to October;
In liquor some take no delight,
    But evermore are sober.
Thus some will cross to Calais, boys,
    While others stop at Dover;
But take my word, if you are wise,
    And go just half-seas over.

    You'll go just half-seas over, boys,
        Go sometimes half-seas over;
    Although the word may seem absurd,
        Go sometimes half-seas over.

I'm not the man to dine or sup
    Without a glass to raise us;

Nor would I deeply drain the cup
   Till mortal made as Blasus.
But when you've swallowed just enough,
   You're like a cow in clover :
How sweet! how snug! when generous stuff
   Has made us half-seas over!
     You'll go just half-seas over, boys, &c.

If maid or widow you would win,
   And wear your wished-for treasure,
You'll find it best to fill your skin
   With just the proper measure.
With less than that to feed your flame,
   You'll prove too cold a lover :
While more might overshoot your aim ;
   So woo her—half-seas over.

    You'll go just half-seas over, boys,
     You'll go just half-seas over;
    With more, or less, you'd miss success,
     So go just half-seas over.

Our friends the French have taught us much
   In cookery and fashions ;
Though all their doings are not such
   As please a Briton's passions.

But Claret good, when rich and true,
    And not, like Gladstone's, *pauvre*—
O! there I like the *Juste milieu*,
    Which means just half-seas over.

It means just half-seas over, boys,
    Precisely half-seas over:
The Juste milieu *is what will do,*
    And means just half-seas over.

A BOTTLE AND FRIEND.

WHEN the evening of life comes with temperate ray
To cool the hot blood that has boiled all the day;
When our faculties flag, and our frolics are o'er,
And our favourite idols are worshipped no more;
May some sober pleasures that season attend,
And Fortune still leave us—a Bottle and Friend.

When Beauty grows shy, and don't think it worth while
On an agèd admirer to lavish a smile:
When we, too, are backward, where oft we were bold,
And don't fall in love once a-week as of old;
As some compensation, may Providence send,
To warm our cold bosoms—a Bottle and Friend.

When even Ambition has ceased to ensnare,
And we're calmly content to remain what we are:
When the Passions die out, of their fuel bereft,
And Ill-nature and Avarice only are left;
From Age and its evils our breasts to defend,
You'll find the best buckler—a Bottle and Friend.

Philosophers say, that the most of mankind,
In the things that they pray for, are foolish and blind;
That what seems a blessing oft turns out a bane,
And that Pleasure is merely the prelude to Pain:
But thus far our wishes may surely extend,
That there ne'er may be wanting—a Bottle and Friend.

THE PLANTING OF THE VINE.

A RABBINICAL LEGEND.

Air—*The year that's awa'*.

WHEN Noah first planted the Vine,
   The Devil contrived to be there,
For he saw pretty well that the Finding of Wine
   Was a very important affair.

Mankind had been sober before;
   But had *not* been remarkably good;
And the cold-blooded crew had deserved all the more
   To be deluged and drenched by the Flood.

To assist us in mending our ways,
   And more safely our time to employ,
It was kindly determined to shorten our days,
   And afford us some generous joy.

Then the grape came to gladden man's heart;
   And a bright dawn of bliss seems to glow,

When the rainbow and wine-cup the tidings impart,
    Of an end both to Water and Woe.

So to hallow the newly-found fruit,
    Noah chose a white Lamb without spot;
And he poured its young blood round the delicate root,
    To preserve it from blemish and blot.

But the Devil, such bounty to clog,
    And to substitute evil for good,
Slaughtered also a Lion, an Ape, and a Hog,
    And manured the young plant with their blood.

The first gush of the Vine's precious balm
    Shows its power in an innocent way:
Like the Lamb's gentle nature, our temper is calm,
    While our spirits are playful and gay.

But on tasting more freely the cup,
    There its Leonine vices are found;
With a combative ardour the heart is lit up,
    And resentment and wrath hover round.

Next, the Ape, if still deeper we drink,
    Its grimaces and gambols will try;

Till at last, like the Hog, oversated we sink,
   And contented lie down in the sty.

In avoiding these villanous beasts,
   Let our sense of the blessing be shown:
Let the Lamb's playful spirit preside at our feasts,
   Nor let even the Lion be known.

But I would not be ruthlessly told
   From all temperate draughts to refrain;
Lest perhaps, like the sober transgressors of old,
   We should bring down the Deluge again.

GASTER, THE FIRST M.A.

"The ruler of this place was one Master Gaster, the first Master of Arts in the world."—RABELAIS.

THERE'S a comical fellow that all of us know,
And who always is with us wherever we go;
But our constant companion and guide though he be,
Yet our eyes never saw him, and never will see.
Of science the source, and of Arts the first Master,—
The name of this wonderful fellow is Gaster.

Search history through with attention and skill,
And you'll find him still busy for good or for ill.
With his mischievous doings you early may grapple
In the old and unhappy affair of the Apple.
Though the Serpent's designs chiefly caused that disaster,
The Serpent was greatly assisted by Gaster.

But when Man was then sentenced to trouble and toil,
It was Gaster that taught him to labour the soil—
To dig and to delve, and to plant for his diet;
And he never would let him a moment be quiet.

Despotic and stern, and a rigid taskmaster,
But an excellent friend and instructor, was Gaster.

After living some ages on water and greens,
Gaster found out that bacon ate nicely with beans;
And he also found out that, to moisten such food,
Something better than water was needful and good.
The Nymph of the Well owned that Bacchus surpassed her,
And gave way to the Grape as the liquor for Gaster.

Now baking, and brewing, and hunting, and fishing
Arose from what Gaster was wanting or wishing.
The grain in the furrow, the fruit on the tree,
The flocks on the mountain, the herds on the lee,
All acknowledged his sway; never empire was vaster
Than the fertile dominions thus subject to Gaster.

Geometry sprang from the Nile's spreading flood,
Just that Gaster might know where his landmarks had stood;
And Commerce grew busy by land and by sea,
Just that Gaster at home well-provisioned might be.
See! the camel, the car, the canoe, the three-master,
All speed with their loads on the missions of Gaster.

Then cities were built with their shops and their houses,
Where in plenty and peace Gaster feasts and carouses;
And a half of the houses and shops in a town,
If great Gaster were gone, might as well be pulled down:
So splendid and spacious on pier and pilaster
Rise the halls we've erected in honour of Gaster.

But I ought to observe that the changes thus made
For the most part took place with Dame Poverty's aid:
For Gaster and She, you don't need me to mention,
Are the father and mother of every invention.
When the pockets contain not a single piaster,
The wits become sharp in the service of Gaster.

I own we've had bloodshed by Gaster's advice,
And proceedings besides that were not over-nice.
Neither Rob Roy nor Cacus had been such a thief,
Hadn't Gaster been always so partial to beef.
When the Mosstrooper's wife saw he'd soon be a faster,
She served up his spurs at the bidding of Gaster.

Yet if Gaster would stay in his natural state,
His exactions would seldom be grievous or great.
But Luxury comes with suggestions officious,
And Cookery tempts him with dishes delicious,

And the Doctor's called in, with his rhubarb and castor,
To remove the sad ills of poor surfeited Gaster.

O! close upon frenzy the maladies border
That Gaster begets when he's long out of order.
Like madmen we hurry, in hopes of release,
To Malvern or Homburg, to Gully or Spiess;
When perhaps the disease would be put to flight faster,
If we just stayed at home and did justice to Gaster.

Try always to suit Gaster's wants to a tittle,
Nor supply his demands with too much or too little.
You will ne'er put a sick man in hearty condition,
If Gaster won't join and assist the physician.
In vain to a wound you'll apply salve or plaster,
If you don't take the pains to conciliate Gaster.

When Beauty puts forth all its glory and grace,
And unites the full splendour of form and of face;
When each gesture is joyous, each movement is light,
And the glance of the eye is serene and yet bright;
When the rose-hue of health tints the pure alabaster,—
Let us own that 'tis partly the doing of Gaster.

Nay, even in your noblest possession, the Mind,
Your dependence on Gaster too often you find.

A redundant repast, a rich supper or *soirée*,
Will oppress the *divinæ particulam auræ;*
While at times, we may see, no professor or pastor
Teaches kindness and charity better than Gaster.

Oft when petty annoyances ruffle the soul,
And the temper defies philosophic control,
The commotion is quelled, and a calm will succeed,
Through the simple device of inhaling the Weed :
Such magical power has the soothing Canaster
To bring balmy content and good-humour to Gaster.

As for me, who thus venture his praise to proclaim,
And adorn his high worth with his classical name,
Let me hope from my patron these verses may bring
Some appropriate boon to assist me to sing ;
For it must be confessed that the poor poetaster
Finds always his best inspiration in Gaster.

October 1862.

NOTE.—If Gaster, as Rabelais says, was a Master of Arts, it seems a precedent for Female Graduation, as Gaster in Greek is feminine.

GASTER.

(ADAPTED TO MUSIC.)

Air—*The Rogue's March.*

IN a far distant age
   (*Vide* Rabelais' page)
Lived a fellow, of Arts the first Master:
   And if further you seek,
   I can tell you in Greek,
That the name of this fellow was Gaster.
   An ingenious fellow was Gaster,
   Though he caused us a little disaster:
     For if you'll look in
     To our first parents' sin,
It was partly the greed of this Gaster.

   Thence into the world,
   Out of paradise hurled,
Adam found here a rigid taskmaster,

Who compelled him to work
Like a Trojan or Turk,
To provide a subsistence for Gaster:
O! a terrible fellow was Gaster:
Whose demands became vaster and vaster:
Man was destined to toil,
And to grub at the soil,
That there might be some grub to give Gaster.

When the infant first thought
How his milk could be brought
From its fountain of fair alabaster,
The nice milking machine
We so often have seen,
Was found out for the service of Gaster.
O! Science must bend before Gaster,
Who in talent has often surpassed her:
Ere we knew what the cause
Of a Vacuum was,
It was made by a baby for Gaster.

Man, after the Flood,
Took to animal food,
As to which he had been a strict faster
And strong meat made him long
To have liquor as strong,
So the grape was fermented for Gaster.

'Twas a perilous crisis for Gaster,
Who began after this to live faster;
   But provided he stop
   At a moderate drop,
It may prove a good cordial for Gaster.

   And still, at this day,
   Gaster figures away,
Our adviser, our guide, our schoolmaster;
   For the most things we do
   Have one object in view—
To provide a good dinner for Gaster.
   Trade and Commerce are fostered by Gaster:
   The skiff, and the lofty three-master,
     Spread abroad their white sail
     To each varying gale,
To bring victuals and drink to friend Gaster.

   But it makes me quite grave,
   To think how we behave,
When we do not our appetites master;
   For we eat, and we swill,
   Twice as much as our fill,
Till we smother and suffocate Gaster.
   Then the Doctor is sent for to Gaster,
   Who prescribes for him rhubarb and castor;

And so dose after dose
In and out of us goes,
To redress the distempers of Gaster.

A connection most rare
Binds the Siamese pair,
More completely than Pollux and Castor;
So the body and soul
Can each other control,
And the mind sympathises with Gaster.
A proper attention to Gaster,
Saves many a potion and plaster:
Even Surgeons have found
That they can't heal a wound,
If they don't first propitiate Gaster.

Would you know the Chief Good
Men so much have pursued,
Since the era of old Zoroaster;
'Tis a conscience serene,
Hands and tongue that are clean,
And a healthy condition of Gaster.
Then fill up a bumper to Gaster:
Not forgetting the poor poetaster,
Who has lent you his time
For this doggerel rhyme,
As a small panegyric on Gaster.

BEEF AND POTATOES.

A DIETETIC DITTY.

Air—*Potatoes grow in Limerick.*

"POTATOES grow in Limerick and beef in Ballimore;"
Use the two together, and of strength you'll have a store:
Beef supplies the fibre, while the *taties* feed the fire;
And a little glass of good poteen will merriment inspire.

Every muscle as it moves some tear and wear sustains;
And thus set free, the old debris find out their several drains:
However sad the thought may seem, the fact is very clear,
That day by day we waste away, and soon should disappear.

But food is sent, with kind intent, the fabric to restore;
The pot that boils our bit of beef rebuilds us as before:

Or should we take, for England's sake, her roast beef so renowned,
You would not wish a nobler dish, with pudding duly browned.

A round of beef in winter time is found a joyous treat,
When pickled with a mixture where both salt and sugar meet :
But salting needs correction, and Old Custom tells the means,
That the round should be encircled with a lively wreath of *greens*.

As some relief, when tired of beef, you'll find that mutton's good ;
With turnips and with caper sauce, it makes a pleasant food :
Mutton old and claret good were Caledonia's forte,
Before the Southron taxed her drink and poisoned her with port.

If fowl or veal should be your meal, then have a slice of ham,
Where fat and lean, together seen, may save an extra dram :

But let your ham be duly boiled, and don't eat pork that's raw,
For fear this Trichiniasis should clutch you in its claw.

Some, *veluti in speculum*, survey their loss and gain,
And try by weight and measure nice a medium to maintain:
So when of all their goings-out they've found the just amount,
They eat, or starve, as best may serve to balance the account.*

But, sooth to say, a simpler way will do the job as well;
Your appetite, if tight and right, will be your dinner-bell;
Eat whene'er you're hungry, and when hunger ceases—stop;
And drink for love and friendship's sake a not immoderate drop.

O happy he, from Doctors free, who thus adjusts his fare,
As true and pat as if he sat in great Santorio's chair!
He doesn't take too little, and he doesn't take too much,
And a heart more sound will not be found, "from Canada to Cutch."

* See 'Spectator,' No. 25.

A SONG OF PROVERBS.

Air—*Push about the jorum.*

IN ancient days, tradition says,
    When knowledge much was stinted—
When few could teach and fewer preach,
    And books were not yet printed—
What wise men thought, by prudence taught,
    They pithily expounded;
And proverbs sage, from age to age,
    In every mouth abounded.

    O blessings on the men of yore,
       Who wisdom thus augmented,
    And left a store of easy lore
       For human use invented.

Two of a trade, 'twas early said,
    Do very ill agree, sir;
A beggar hates at rich men's gates
    A beggar's face to see, sir.

Yet trades there are, though rather rare,
    Where men are not so jealous;
Two lawyers know the coal to blow,
    Just like a pair of bellows.

    O blessings, &c.

When tinkers try their trade to ply,
    They make more holes than mend, sir;
Set some astride a horse to ride,
    You know their latter end, sir.
Rogues meet their due when out they fall,
    And each the other blames, sir;
The pot should not the kettle call
    Opprobious sorts of names, sir.

    O blessings, &c.

The man who would Charybdis shun,
    Must make a cautious movement,
Or else he'll into Scylla run—
    Which would be no improvement.
The fish that left the frying-pan,
    On feeling that desire, sir,
Took little by their change of plan,
    When floundering in the fire, sir.

    O blessings, &c.

A man of nous from a glass house
    Will not be throwing stones, sir;
A mountain may bring forth a mouse,
    With many throes and groans, sir.
A friend in need's a friend indeed,
    And prized as such should be, sir;
But summer friends, when summer ends,
    Are off and o'er the sea, sir.
      O blessings, &c.

Sour grapes, we cry, of things too high,
    Which gives our pride relief, sir;
Between two stools the bones of fools
    Are apt to come to grief, sir.
Truth, some folks tell, lies in a well,
    Though why I ne'er could see, sir;
But some opine 'tis found in wine,
    Which better pleases me, sir.
      O blessings, &c.

Your toil and pain will all be vain,
    To try to milk the bull, sir;
If forth you jog to shear the hog,
    You'll get more cry than wool, sir.
'Twould task your hand to sow the sand,
    Or shave a chin that's bare, sir;

A Song of Proverbs.

You cannot strip a Highland hip
  Of what it does not wear, sir.
    O blessings, &c.

Of proverbs in the common style
  If now you're growing weary,
I'll try again to raise a smile
  With two by Lord Dundreary.
You cannot brew good Burgundy
  Out of an old sow's ear, sir;
Nor can you make a silken purse
  From very sour small beer, sir.
    O blessings, &c.

Now he who listens to my song,
  And heeds what I indite, sir,
Will seldom very far go wrong,
  And often will go right, sir.
But whoso hears with idle ears,
  And is no wiser made, sir,
A fool is he, and still would be,
  Though in a mortar brayed, sir.
    O blessings, &c.

January 1864.

A SONG OF TRUISMS.

Air—*Vivan tutte.*

HARK to me, and I will tell you
    Some things you may find of value:
Common-sense and useful knowledge
Are not only got at College.

    This is true beyond a doubt,
    Whosoever found it out.

Soldiers fight and fall in battle;
Calves and cows are counted cattle;
Sheep make turnips into mutton;
Fat men's clothes don't freely button.

    This is true, &c.

Oxygen combines with iron;
Marvels great our lives environ;
I've seen human bears and monkeys,
Plumeless geese and two-legged donkeys.

    This is true, &c.

A Song of Truisms.

Ducks and Dutchmen love aquatics;
Some poor people live in attics;
Some set order at defiance;
Some believe in Social Science.

    This is true, &c.

Chance and change are never ceasing;
Moons keep waning and increasing;
Here the Pope fresh power is getting;
There, abroad, his sun is setting.

    This is true, &c.

One Extreme begets another;
Day and Night are child and mother;
Misers' sons soon spend their money;
Comic songs are far from funny.

    This is true, &c.

Wrinkles aren't cured by riches;
Some wives wear their husbands' breeches;
Beauties like to have their roses
Rather on their cheeks than noses.

    This is true, &c.

Venison makes a noble pasty;
What is cheap is often nasty;
'Tis a project quite Utopian
To wash white an Ethiopian.

    This is true, &c.

If you wish to hear related
All the truths that could be stated,
I might thus go on till supper,
Near as wise as Martin Tupper.

    This is true beyond a doubt,
    But your patience now is out.

SONG AT THE SYMPOSIUM ON MAGA.

Air—*The Arethusa.*

COME, all good friends who stretch so free
    Your legs beneath our Ebony,
In loving lays along with me,
   Proclaim the praise of Maga.
She is a creature not too good
For human nature's daily food:
   And her men are stanch to their favourite haunch,
   On which they fall like an avalanche,
   And fairly floor it, root and branch,
    In the name of mighty Maga.

'Tis sweet to see, when hard at work,
These heroes armed with knife and fork,
While flashes far the frequent cork
   To refresh the thirst of Maga.
Some dozen dishes swept away
Are but the prologue to our play:

If a haunch can't be found upon English ground,
Then the best of blackfaced, duly browned,
Or the faultless form of a well-fed round,
   Must sustain the strength of Maga.

Our banquet, lately spread to view,
Appears to me an emblem true
Of that served up in season due
   To the monthly guests of Maga.
No rival feast can e'er compare
With Maga's mental bill of fare,
   While her table is gay with a French fricassée,
   A currie, casserole, or a cabriolet,*
   Yet solid substance still bears sway
      In the rich repasts of Maga.

How many myriad mouths attend
Till Maga's hand their meat shall send!
What scholars, poets, patriots, bend
   Their eager eyes on Maga!
The knock that speaks a Number come,
Stirs the soldier's heart like the sound of a drum;
   While with pallid cheer, between hope and fear,
   Fair maidens ask, " Pray, does there appear

---

* A convenient name for any dish that has no other name.

Song at the Symposium on Maga.

Any more this month of Ten Thousand a-Year,
   In the pleasing page of Maga?"

What fleets of Granton steamers sail,
Each laden with our monthly bale,
Besides that part that goes by rail,
   Of the wondrous works of Maga!
O'er all the earth, what scene or soil
Is not found full of Maga's toil?
   Every varying breeze wafts her over the seas,
   While insurance at Lloyd's is done with ease
   At nothing per cent, or what you please,
     On the craft that carries Maga.

Survey mankind with careful view,
From Cochin-China to Peru,
And take a transverse section too;
   All read and reverence Maga.
Around the poles, beneath the line,
She rules and reigns by right divine;
   She is thought no sin by Commissioner Lin;
   And, waiving at once the point of Pin,
   The Celestial Empire all take in
     The barbarian Mouth of Maga.

But most her page can joy impart
To many a home-sick Scottish heart,
That owns afar the potent art
   Possessed by mighty Maga.
The exile sees, at her command,
His native mountains round him stand;
  In vision clear his home is near,
  And a murmuring streamlet fills his ear;
  Till now the fast o'erflowing tear
   Dissolves the spell of Maga.

But next let North inspire the strain :
Ye Muses, ope your richest vein!
Though flattery goes against the grain
   With the master-mind of Maga.
Without him all to wreck would run :
A system then without a sun !
  For his eye and soul, with strong control,
  Enlighten all that round him roll,
  And gild and guide the mighty whole,
   That bears the name of Maga.

Then, now before we bid adieu,
We wish, while yet the year is new,

Succeeding seasons, not a few,
   To the noble North and Maga.
May life's best gifts their progress bless!
May their lights—and their shadows—never be less!
   May they lengthen their lease with an endless increase!
   Or only then depart in peace,
   When frauds shall fail and follies cease,
     Subdued by North and Maga.

February 1841.

HILLI-ONNEE.

[*In the year* 1841 *Lord Palmerston had a celebrated race-horse called Ilione, the pronunciation of whose name became a matter of dispute on the turf. An appeal having been made to his lordship, he replied, to the surprise of some scholars, that it should be pronounced as if written* Hillionnee. *Apparently this view arose from his lordship's having become a convert to the system of accentual pronunciation. The ordinary English mode of pronouncing the name is that indicated by Pitt in his translation of the Eneid, Book I., when he speaks of the sceptre*

"That wont Ilione's fair hand to grace."]

THE Whigs can boast of many a name,
    Great Normanby and Little Johnny;
But far their foremost child of fame
    Is he that owns fleet Hilli-onnee.

'Mong lords and legs a contest rose
    As fierce as e'er we fought with Bonny:
From words it almost came to blows,
    And still the theme was Hilli-onnee.

And some said this, and some said that;
    No want there was of caco-phony:

Hilli-onnee.

With short and long, with sharp and flat,
   They sore misnomered Hilli-onnee.

Then one bethought him of a way
   To terminate this acri-mony;
He called as umpire of the fray,
   The lord that owns fleet Hilli-onnee.

His lordship, though a scholar once,
   At this appeal was much *étonné;*
But loath to be esteemed a dunce,
   He searched his books for Hilli-onnee.

No doubt he well remembered yet
   Old Sophocles's *Hanti-gonnee;*
A clearer case he could not get,
   Nor more in point for Hilli-onnee.

But firmer proofs he sought and found;
   The Greeks, disliking mono-tonny.
Had accents to direct the sound,
   And these showed here 'twas Hilli-onnee.

He wrote his answer, brief, yet bright
   With classic wit and keen i-ronny,

And having quashed the Tories quite,
    He taught us all 'twas Hilli-onnee.

O Peel! your guilt what tongue can tell!
    'Twas nothing less than rank fe-lonny,
To oust a lord who talks so well
    Of heathen Greek and Hilli-onnee.

Had I the might of Pindar's muse
    To sing the praise of Palmer-stonny;
The deathless prince of Syracuse
    Should yield to him and Hilli-onnee.

Pindar, alas! is in his grave;
    But this good page of old E-bonny,
For distant days the names shall save
    Of Palmer-ston and Hilli-onnee.

November 1841.

THE THREE R'S.

YOU must own, Mrs Bull, that your family's large,
    Say, some two or three millions at least;
And so many small children must prove a great charge,
    Which of late has been strangely increased.
To their schooling, of course, we must carefully see,
    Or a slur on us both it will fling;
But, as all of the lot cannot gentlefolks be,
    Why, I think, the three R's is the thing.

One lad must be keeping the cow from the corn,
    Or must wait on the wandering sheep:
Another must double Cape Wrath or Cape Horn—
    A cabin-boy far on the deep.
As soon as the plumes on their pinions grow strong,
    From the nest they are sure to take wing;
So their time with the schoolmaster cannot be long,
    And 'tis clear the three R's is the thing.

To read well their Bible, to write to a friend,
    And to cast up a common account,

This is easily taught, and though this were the end,
  'Tis a boon of no slender amount.
Would they learn Mathematics, or Grammar, or Greek,
  E'en supposing we gave them their swing?
Or would these make them fitter a service to seek?
  No, no; the three R's is the thing.

Would you deck out a daughter in satin and silk,
  Who must work for the bread she's to eat?
Would you send out your maids to the cow-house to milk,
  With fine kid-leather shoes on their feet?
Should your ploughboys, like folks at the playhouse, be dressed,
  As if only to dance and to sing?
No! such tawdry attire would but make them a jest:
  So, again, the three R's is the thing.

Then, my dear, there's a matter I've lately observed,
  Makes me sorely our system distrust:
'Tis that some boys are stuffed, while the others are starved,
  Which is cruel as well as unjust.

To the general mass, to the average class,
  We should knowledge and nourishment bring:
Give them plain wholesome fare, but let each have a
    share;
And for *that* the three R's is the thing.

1862.

O WHY SHOULD A WOMAN NOT GET A DEGREE?

ON FEMALE GRADUATION AND LADIES' LECTURES.

Air—Argyll is my name.

YE fusty old fogies, Professors by name,
    A deed you've been doing of sorrow and shame:
Though placed in your Chairs to spread knowledge abroad,
Against half of mankind you would shut up the road:
College honours and lore from the Fair you withdraw,
By enforcing against them a strict Salic law:
Is it fear? is it envy? or what can it be?
And why should a woman not get a degree?

How ungrateful of You, whose best efforts depend
On the aid certain Ladies in secret may send:
CLIO *here* writes a lecture, URANIA *there*,
And more Muses than one prompt the Musical Chair.
CALLIOPE sheds o'er the Classics delight,
And the lawyers have meetings with THEMIS by night;

O why should a Woman not get a Degree?

Yet, if VENUS de' Medici came, even She
Could among her own Medici get no degree.

In Logic a woman may seldom excel;
But in Rhetoric always she bears off the bell.
Fair PORTIA will show woman's talent for law,
When in old Shylock's bond she could prove such a flaw.
She would blunder in Physic no worse than the rest,
She could leave things to Nature as well as the best;
She could feel at your wrist, she could finger your fee;
Then why should a woman not get a degree?

Your tardy repentance now seeks to supply
What your jealousy formerly dared to deny.
You would open a byway where women may *pass*,
And by which, if they can, they may climb to a *class*.
But you seem to exact intellectual riches,
Such as only are found with the wearers of breeches:
So if I were to marry, the woman for Me
Shouldn't try for a Class, or desire a degree.

Your Lectures for Ladies some fruit may produce;
For a Course of good lectures is always of use.
On a married Professor your choice should alight,
Who may lecture by day—as he's lectured at night.

And allow me to ask, what would Husbands become,
If they weren't well lectured by women at home?
When from faults and from follies men thus are kept free,
There surely the woman deserves a degree.

Yet without a degree see how well the Sex knows
How to bind up our wounds and to lighten our woes!
They need *no* Doctor's gown their fair limbs to enwrap,
They need ne'er hide their locks in a Graduate's cap.
Then I wonder a woman, the Mistress of Hearts,
Would descend to aspire to be Master of Arts :
A Ministering Angel in Woman we see,
And an Angel should covet no other Degree.

THE READING OF GREEK.

A SONG FOR A HELLENIC CLUB.

Air—*Lillibulero.*

THIS life is a medley of good and of ill,
    A strange alternation of joy and of grief;
Its maladies baffle both potion and pill,
    Yet I've found out a cure that will give us relief.
        Its aid if you borrow,
        'Twill banish your sorrow,
And brighten your path when the prospect is bleak;
        In short, it will be a
        Complete panacea—
And it simply consists in the Reading of Greek.

The worst of our evils spring out of the mind—
    We're proud and resentful, we're sordid and vain;
Take a course of my medicine, and quickly you'll find,
    Of every such ailment you'll cease to complain.
        A winter and summer
        Of Plato and Homer

Will make you quite strong where at present you're weak;
  With you or your daughters,
  The Kissingen waters
Might well be exchanged for the Reading of Greek.

If rage and revenge are the bane of your life,
 In the wrath of Achilles a beacon you'll see;
If you'd be a good husband and cherish your wife,
 Ulysses and Hector your models may be.
  The foul-mouthed Thersites
  So brimful of spite is
That nobody here to be like him would seek;
  While the beautiful Helen
  A story is telling
That reads us a lesson in Reading our Greek.

The truths that old Homer so gloriously sung,
 The spirit of Plato as nobly has said;
The sweets of Hymettus distil from his tongue,
 And a half-divine halo encircles his head.
  Of love and of beauty,
  Of drinking and duty,
He makes his own Socrates worthily speak;
  The famous old codger,
  A regular dodger,
Will teach you some tricks in your Reading of Greek.

The Reading of Greek.

What follies some wise-looking people commit,
   Whose fault is a thickness of blood or of skull!
Impervious to laughter and proof against wit,
   Their dreary existence flows ditch-like and dull.
      Now there's nothing on earth, sir,
      Conduces to mirth, sir,
Like the Old Comic vein of fun, frolic, and freak;
      And although to our cost, sir,
      Margites is lost, sir,
Aristophanes lives for our Reading in Greek.

Then see how around us there everywhere reigns
   A shopkeeping spirit so keen and intense,
That nobody's valued except for his gains,
   And all things are weighed by pounds, shillings, and pence!
      With a view to abate, sir,
      A nuisance so great, sir,
And Parliament purge of the huckstering clique,
      I'd make every new Member,
      Each month of November,
Pass through Donaldson's* hands for the Reading of Greek.

---

* Dr Donaldson, at one time an Examiner for the University, now Rector of the High School of Edinburgh.

To you, my fair friends, let me now recommend
    The charming example of Lady Jane Grey:
To the good of both sexes such conduct would tend,
    For lovers will follow where you lead the way.
        In the gaily-filled ball-room,
        Or pleasanter small room,
The blush would be brought to the dandy's pale cheek,
        If his partner would try him
        With Paris and Priam,
And hackle him well on the Reading of Greek.

What a blest Revolution we then should behold,
    When true Wisdom and Wit had enlivened us all!
When the Good and the Fair should their treasures unfold,
    And the three-volume Novel should go to the Wall.
        But don't overdo it;
        Bring Common-sense to it:
No pedants in petticoats here I'd bespeak:
        But let household employments,
        And social enjoyments,
Alternate bear sway with the Reading of Greek.

HOW TO MAKE A NOVEL.

A SENSATIONAL SONG.

Air—*Bob and Joan.*

TRY with me and mix
    What will make a Novel,
All hearts to transfix
    In house or hall or hovel.
Put the caldron on,
    Set the bellows blowing,
We'll produce anon
    Something worth the showing.
      Toora-loora-loo, &c.

Never mind your *plot;*
    'Tisn't worth the trouble:
Throw into the pot
    What will boil and bubble.
Character's a jest;
    What's the use of study?

All will stand the test
   That's black enough and bloody.
  Toora-loora, &c.

Here's the 'Newgate Guide,'
   Here's the 'Causes Célèbres;'
Tumble in beside,
   Pistol, gun, and sabre.
These Police reports,
   Those Old Bailey trials,
Horrors of all sorts,
   To match the Seven Vials.*

  ✣ *Toora-loora*, &c.

Down into a well,
   Lady, thrust your lover;
Truth as some folks tell,
   There he may discover.
Stepdames, sure though slow,
   Rivals of your daughters,
Bring us from below
   Styx and all its waters.

  Toora-loora, &c,

  ✣ Seven Dials?—*Printer's Devil.*

Crime, that breaks all bounds,
    Bigamy and arson;
Poison, blood, and wounds,
    Will carry well the farce on.
Now it's just in shape;
    Yet, with fire and murder,
Treason, too, and rape
    Might help it all the further.

    Toora-loora, &c.

Or, by way of change,
    In your wild narration
Choose adventures strange
    Of fraud and personation.
Make the job complete;
    Let your vile assassin
Rob and forge and cheat,
    For his victim passin'.

    Toora-loora, &c.

Tame is Virtue's school;
    Paint, as more effective,
Villain, knave, and fool,
    With always a Detective.

Hate for Love may sit;
   Gloom will do for Gladness,
Banish Sense and Wit,
   And dash in lots of Madness.
    Toora-loora, &c.

Stir the broth about;
   Keep the furnace glowing:
Soon we'll pour it out
   In three bright volumes flowing.
Some may jeer and jibe;
   We know where the Shop is,
Ready to subscribe
   For a thousand copies!

    Toora-loora-loo,
    Toora-loora-leddy;
    Now the dish will do,
    Now the Novel's ready!

AD SODALITATIS HELLENICÆ SOCIOS,

CARMEN

MELODIÆ APTATUM SCOTICÆ,

Cui titulus—*O'er the Muir among the Heather.*

CELEBREMUS, O! sodales,
    Noctes has conviviales:
Vel legendo, vel bibendo,
Non invenietis tales.

Libri Græci hic volvuntur:
Fratres legunt et loquuntur:
Ridet jocus; adest coquus;
Et liquores consumuntur.

Ut perfecta sit doctrina,
Magnam opem fert culina:
Is qui sapit cœnam capit,
Et prudenter sumit vina.

Hæ sunt epulæ divinæ,
Ala, pectus, crus,—gallinæ :
Fricta frusta, blanda crusta,
Ostreæque submarinæ.

Interim invadit sitis,
Quæ levatur fructu vitis,
Vel Hispano, vel Germano,
Dum sit fortis et sit mitis.

At quum dapes sunt finitæ,
Gutta parva aquæ vitæ
Dat calorem, dat vigorem,
Saltem si sit mixta ritè.

Hæ dum voluptates placent,
Carmina non spreta jacent :
Sic impleti, sumus læti,
Et Camænæ raro tacent.

Quum receptum jam sit satis
Vini, cibi, græcitatis,
His pro donis, O! quam bonis,
Gratias agamus Fatis.

Ad Sodalitatis Hellenicæ Socios.

Quisque tunc ad suum tectum
Abeat, et petat lectum;
Ut profundo et jucundo
Corpus somno sit refectum.

Magnum denique clamorem,
Hujus cœtûs in honorem,
Excitemus, et laudemus
Clarum ejus Fundatorem.

NOTE.—*Conviviales*, it is believed, would be a better word in the second line than *conviviales*, if it would only sing and sound as well. But the Latinity of the song throughout is not meant to be warranted as rising above that standard which goes by the name of Canine.

THE PROPOSAL OF POLTYS.

Πόλτυς, ὁ Θρᾳκῶν Βασιλεὺς, ἐν τῷ Τρωϊκῷ πολέμῳ, πρεσβευσαμένων πρὸς αὐτὸν ἅμα τῶν Τρώων καὶ τῶν Ἀχαιῶν, ἐκέλευσε τὸν Ἀλέξανδρον, ἀποδόντα τὴν Ἑλένην, δύο παρ' αυτοῦ λαβεῖν καλὰς γυναῖκας.

PLUTARCHI *Apophthegmata.**

Air—*O! London is a fine town.*

O! POLTYS was a man of peace, and loved a quiet life;
His neighbours, too, he tried to keep from bloodshed and from strife.
He flourished in the famous times that saw the Trojan war,
But held aloof from war's alarms, and viewed the fight afar.

The Trojans, and the Grecians too, by every trick did try
To win o'er Poltys to their side, and make him an ally:

---

* See also Prior's 'Alma.'

For Poltys was a king of Thrace, and lived betwixt the two,
And embassies arrived to him with every wind that blew.

But Poltys said: "The case is this, that Paris, that young scamp,
Has wheedled Menelaus' wife, and got her to decamp:
And Menelaus wants her back, though I would not do so,
For when a wife resolves to run, I'd always let her go.

"Yet I've a plan by which, I think, much mischief may be saved,
For I've two comely Wives to spare, extremely well-behaved.
These dames on Paris I'll bestow, if Helen he'll restore;
And if he is not quite a fool, he'll never ask for more.

"He likes the wives of other men, but here are two for one;
And surely that's a fair exchange, so then the thing is done.
The man will have his mare again, and strife and trouble cease,
And all of you, and Poltys too, may live and die in peace."

This plan, no doubt, if followed out, had saved much grief and wrong;
But Homer would have wanted then the subject of his song.
He never would have Hector known, or heard of Andro-màchè,*
Might ne'er have been *traduced* by Pope, or *overset* by Blackie.

And then if Homer had not sung, we might have had no Greek,
And Plato and the Stagyrite might still have been to seek.
A poet Virgil ne'er had been but for his predecessor,
And where were modern Athens now without her Greek Professor?

Then though so many heroes fell upon the Trojan plain,
The Iliad and the Odyssey have made the loss a gain;
And that old Maxim may be true, by some so stoutly pressed,
That on the whole, and in the end, WHATEVER IS IS BEST.

* See Swift.

THE PENNY OF PASES.

Pasetis semiobolus.—EX ERASMI ADAGIIS.
Tradunt Pasetem quendam præstigiarum et magiæ peritiâ primum nomen meruisse.—Emebat autem frequenter, pretiumque rei numerabat: verum mox nummus, non apud venditorem, sed apud Pasetem, reperiebatur.—SIC ETIAM APUD SUIDAM VO. *Pases.*

AIR—*Abraham Newland.*

WHAT ills we endure
    When condemned to be poor,
Doesn't need to be told in fine phrases;
    Nor how matters would mend
    Were a Fairy our friend,
Who would give us the Penny of Pases.
O! for the Penny of Pases!
The miraculous Penny of Pases!
    When he paid it away,
    Ere a word you could say,
It was back in the pocket of Pases.

It is certain that many
By turning a penny
Get wealth that all people amazes:
And so We might grow rich,
To a wonderful pitch,
Just by turning the Penny of Pases.
The astonishing Penny of Pases!
I can never enough sing its praises;
No figures could count
The prodigious amount
We might raise by the Penny of Pases.

But I wouldn't as yet
Pay the National debt,
Which I think one of Stuart Mill's crazes;
Nor in luxury wallow,
And guzzle and swallow
All I got from the Penny of Pases.
When I think of the Penny of Pases,
My breast with benevolence blazes:
Such good I would do,
Such fine projects pursue,
When possessed of the Penny of Pases.

Men of wit and of worth,
The true salt of the earth,
Then should ride in their coaches and chaises;

The Penny of Pases.

    All moneyless merit
    Should freely inherit
A share of my Penny of Pases.
With the help of the Penny of Pases.
The beef of yon bullock that grazes
    Should soon fatten all those
    Who walk loose in their clo'es
For want of the Penny of Pases.

    I would lavish my dollars
    On Poets and Scholars;
I'd put Art on a liberal basis:
    Scientific Inventors
    Should hold some debentures
To be paid from my Penny of Pases.
The Church, too, should profit by Pases
(If it shun all Papistical phases):
    Poor Curates with charges
    Should taste of my largess,
Enriched by the Penny of Pases.

    I would portion young girls
    Who would keep their own curls,
And who wouldn't wear chignons or jaseys;
    And, in spite of their dads,
    I would teach little lads
Some things well worth the Penny of Pases.

If I had but the Penny of Pases,
I would strew life's hard pathway with daisies:
    The Saturnian reign
    Should be brought back again,
By the use of the Penny of Pases.

But a Voice seems to ask,
"Are You fit for this task?"
And a delicate question it raises;
    For I freely confess
    One might make a sad mess,
Misapplying the Penny of Pases.
If we look at life's intricate mazes,
Perhaps he who piously gazes
    May a Providence see
    That is wiser than We,
And that needs not the Penny of Pases.

LET US ALL BE UNHAPPY ON SUNDAY.

A LYRIC FOR SATURDAY NIGHT.

Air—*We bipeds made up of frail clay.*

WE zealots, made up of stiff clay,
    The sour-looking children of sorrow,
While not over-jolly to-day,
    Resolve to be wretched to-morrow.
We can't for a certainty tell
    What mirth may molest us on Monday;
But, at least, to begin the week well,
    Let us all be unhappy on Sunday.

That day, the calm season of rest,
    Shall come to us freezing and frigid;
A gloom all our thoughts shall invest,
    Such as Calvin would call over-rigid.
With sermons from morning till night,
    We'll strive to be decent and dreary:
To preachers a praise and delight,
    Who ne'er think that sermons can weary.

All tradesmen cry up their own wares;
   In this they agree well together:
The Mason by stone and lime swears;
   The Tanner is always for leather.
The Smith still for iron would go;
   The Schoolmaster stands up for teaching;
And the Parson would have you to know,
   There's nothing on earth like his preaching.

The face of kind Nature is fair;
   But our system obscures its effulgence:
How sweet is a breath of fresh air!
   But our rules don't allow the indulgence.
These gardens, their walks and green bowers,
   Might be free to the poor man for one day;
But no, the glad plants and gay flowers
   Mustn't bloom or smell sweetly on Sunday.

What though a good precept we strain
   Till hateful and hurtful we make it!
What though, in thus pulling the rein,
   We may draw it so tight as to break it!
Abroad we forbid folks to roam,
   For fear they get social or frisky;
But of course they can sit still at home,
   And get dismally drunk upon whisky.

Let us all be Unhappy on Sunday.

Then, though we can't certainly tell
    How mirth may molest us on Monday;
At least, to begin the week well,
    Let us all be unhappy on Sunday.

THE THREE MODERATORS.

[*Written on the almost simultaneous appearance of three expositions of ecclesiastical views—the Addresses by the Moderators of the Established and Free Church Assemblies of Scotland, and an Allocution at Rome by the Pope on the state of the Catholic Church.*]

AIR—*Abraham Newland.*

WHEN a clerical set
In Assembly are met,
They are apt to prove angry debaters;
So, their wrath to restrain,
And due calmness maintain,
They have men that are called Moderators.
All Churches should have Moderators,
And should choose them of peaceable *naturs;*
Much trouble it saves
When some oil on the waves
Can be poured by your true Moderators.

But this good class of men,
I'm afraid, now and then,

To their office of peace have proved traitors;
And too much, on the whole,
Have kept blowing the coal,
When they ought to have been Moderators.
What a pity that Church Moderators,
Like so many Vesuvian craters,
Should send forth, in their ire,
Thunder, fury, and fire
All around these inflamed Moderators.

I took pains to compare
The harangues from the chair
Lately made by two Reverend Paters;
And I read, the same day,
What the Pope had to say—
For the Popes are just Rome's Moderators.*
The Pope and our two Moderators
Are surely not three Agitators!
Yet it's clear that the *first*,
Who, I hope, is the worst,
Is no model for true Moderators.

One famous divine,
In his humorous line,

* The Pope and Cardinals, in their original constitution, may be said to have been simply the Moderator and Presbytery of Rome, the Cardinals being the supposed clergy of the City Churches.

Could not fail to delight all spectators;
    But some thought to his tongue
    An astringency clung,
Scarcely known to our old Moderators.
The *third* of these same Moderators
I wish may have some imitators :
    For Bisset to me
    Seemed the best of the three,
And comes nearest our true Moderators.

1862

THE TOURIST'S MATRIMONIAL GUIDE THROUGH SCOTLAND.

A NEW SONG.

AIR—*Woo'd and married an' a'.*

YE tourists, who Scotland would enter,
    The summer or autumn to pass,
I'll tell you how far you may venture
    To flirt with your lad or your lass;
How close you may come upon marriage,
    Still keeping the wind of the law,
And not, by some foolish miscarriage,
    Get woo'd and married an' a'.

Woo'd and married an' a';
Married and woo'd an' a':
And not, by some foolish miscarriage,
Get woo'd and married an' a'.

This maxim itself might content ye,
    That marriage is made—by consent;
Provided it's done *de præsenti*,
    And marriage is really what's meant.
Suppose that young Jockey and Jenny
    Say, "We two are husband and wife;"
The witnesses needn't be many—
    They're instantly buckled for life.

    Woo'd and married an' a';
    Married and woo'd an' a':
    It isn't with us a hard thing
    To get woo'd and married an' a'.

Suppose the man only has spoken,
    The woman just giving a nod;
They're spliced by that very same token
    Till one of them's under the sod.
Though words would be bolder and blunter,
    The want of them isn't a flaw;
For *nutu signisque loquuntur*
    Is good Consistorial Law.

    Woo'd and married an' a';
    Married and woo'd an' a':
    A wink is as good as a word
    To get woo'd and married an' a'.

If people are drunk or delirious,
  The marriage of course would be bad ;
Or if they're not sober and serious,
  But acting a play or charade.
It's bad if it's only a cover
  For cloaking a scandal or sin,
And talking a landlady over
  To let the folks lodge in her inn.

> *Woo'd and married an' a';*
> *Married and woo'd an' a':*
> *It isn't the mere use of words*
> *Makes you woo'd and married an' a'.*

You'd better keep clear of love-letters,
  Or write them with caution and care ;
For, faith, they may fasten your fetters,
  If wearing a conjugal air.
Unless you're a knowing old stager,
  'Tis here you'll most likely be lost ;
As a certain much-talked-about Major
  Had very near found to his cost.

> *Woo'd and married an' a';*
> *Married and woo'd an' a':*
> *They are perilous things, pen and ink,*
> *To get woo'd and married an' a'.*

I ought now to tell the unwary,
   That into the noose they'll be led,
By giving a promise to marry,
   And acting as if they were wed.
But if, when the promise you're plighting,
   To keep it you think you'd be loath,—
Just see that it isn't in writing,
   And then it must come to your oath.

> *Woo'd and married an' a';*
> *Married and woo'd an' a':*
> *I've shown you a dodge to avoid*
> *Being woo'd and married an' a'.*

A third way of tying the tether,
   Which sometimes may happen to suit,
Is living a good while together,
   And getting a married repute.
But you who are here as a stranger,
   And don't mean to stay with us long,
Are little exposed to that danger;
   So here I may finish my song.

> *Woo'd and married an' a';*
> *Married and woo'd an' a':*
> *You're taught now to seek or to shun*
> *Being woo'd and married an' a'.*

DECIMIS INCLUSIS.

"*Many lands in Scotland are enjoyed* cum decimis inclusis et nunquam antea separatis. *All our writers agree that such lands are free from the payment of tithes.*"—ERSKINE'S INSTITUTE.

AIR—*Maggie Lauder.*

I'VE often wished it were my fate,
   Enriched by Fortune's bounty,
To own a little nice Estate
   In some delightful county;
Where I, perhaps, with some applause,
   Might cultivate the Muses,
And till my lands, and have a clause
   Cum decimis inclusis.

Wherever no such clause appears,
   You're doomed to much vexation;
The Minister, each twenty years,
   Pursues his augmentation.
Like any fiend he grabs your teind,
   Unless the Court refuses,

And all are sold who do not hold
    Cum decimis inclusis.

That strife to tell, would answer well
    This tune of Maggie Lauder,
When half the Bar are waging war
    About the extra cha'der.
But Outram's wit that scene has hit,
    And all so much amuses,
That I refrain, and turn my strain
    To *decimis inclusis.*

'Twould be a dry and dreary theme,
    With nothing ornamental,
To tell you how the Interim scheme
    Adopts the Proven rental;
The Common agent in the suit,
    Objecting where he chooses,
Is glad when he can well dispute
    Your *decimis inclusis.*

A friend of mine had such a grant,
    And did not get it *gratis;*
But when produced, 'twas found to want
    The *nunquam separatis.*

An Heritor with such a flaw
    His whole exemption loses,
And might as well possess, in law,
    No *decimis inclusis*.

Then ere you buy, your titles try,
    For fear they're in disorder:
An Old Church feu's the thing for you,
    From some Cistercian Order.
Demand a progress stanch and tight,
    For nothing that excuses,
And see your *nunquam antea*'s right,
    As well as your *inclusis*.

Then free from fear and free from strife,
    Your cares and troubles over,
You'll lead a gay and easy life
    Among your corn and clover.
The whole Teind Court you'll make your sport,
    Which else such awe diffuses,
"Augment away," you'll blithely say,
    "I've *decimis inclusis*."

SATURDAY AT E'EN.

AIR—*I gaed a waefu' gate yestreen.*

COME all ye jolly lawyer lads who wrangle for a fee,
Now, lay aside your briefs a while, and sing this song with me:
For it's you, and you alone, can respond to what I mean,
And blithely raise the song in praise of Saturday at e'en.

> *Of Saturday at e'en, boys, of Saturday at e'en;*
> *We'll blithely raise the song in praise of Saturday at e'en.*

Throughout the weary week we work, at morn, at noon, at night,
And spin our restless brains away to make the wrong seem right.
But our troubles and our toils they are all forgotten, clean,
When we broach a flask from Cockburn's cask on Saturday at e'en.

> *On Saturday at e'en,* &c.

Saturday at E'en.

To-night at last the married man enjoys his heart's desire,
And with his wife and children dear surrounds the cheerful fire;
While bachelors repair to some gay and glitt'ring scene,
Or court some bonnie lassie now on Saturday at e'en.

    On Saturday at e'en, &c.

Supremely blest among the rest, the Magnates on the Bench
Can smooth their brow and venture now their ardent thirst to quench:
Even the Junior on the Bills did not stand in awe of Skene,
Nor fears to scan the face of Mann on Saturday at e'en.

    On Saturday at e'en, &c.

But would you know where most I'd go these pleasant hours to pass;
With whom I'd wish to eat my fish, with whom to drink my glass?
It is not with the Advocate, it is not with the Dean,
But it's with some jolly junior lads on Saturday at e'en.

    On Saturday at e'en, &c.

Then come you jolly lawyer lads another bottle draw,
Forget your condescendences, forget your pleas in law;
If any state objections, we'll allow them to be seen,
But we'll meanwhile drain the cup again to Saturday
 at e'en.

> To Saturday at e'en, boys, to Saturday at e'en,
> We'll meanwhile drain the cup again to Saturday at e'en.

O! HE WAS LANG O' COMING.*

Air—*The Auld Wife ayont the fire.*

NED LOTHIAN took a work in hand,
    To spread his fame throughout the land;
And let the lieges understand
    How learnèd was our Lothian.

    But O! he was lang o' coming;
    Very, very lang o' coming:
    Surely he was lang o' coming;
        What could hinder Lothian?

When Lothian did his plan arrange,
    He looked for nothing new or strange:

---

* Mr Edward Lothian, an excellent lawyer and an excellent man, was engaged in writing an Institute of the Law of Scotland; but having kept back his book for more than the Horatian period of gestation (it was never published), a good many changes in the law took place, which, with some anachronisms, are sought to be here represented. It should be added that no one used to enjoy the singing of the song more than the Subject of it.

But ere he finished—what a change!
    How sore perplexed was Lothian!
        But then he was sae lang o' coming, &c.

What powers the Admiral possessed,
And what with Commissaries rest—
Was all most learnedly expressed
    In this great work by Lothian.
        But why was he sae lang o' coming? &c.

How Services should be obtained
Before the Macers, he explained;
No part of this dark theme remained
    Without some light from Lothian.
        But then he was sae lang o' coming, &c.

The Admiralty Court is fled;
The Commissaries—gone to bed;
The Macers knocked upon the head;
    A heavy blow to Lothian!
        But what made him sae lang o' coming? &c.

Election law he grappled fast;
But when he held it at the last,

O! He was Lang o' Coming.

The Scotch Reform Bill had been passed;
    A fearful shock to Lothian!

    But why was he sae lang o' coming? &c.

Of Sasines he had much to say;
But ere his chapter saw the day,
Infeftments all were done away;
    Another loss to Lothian!

    But then he was sae lang o' coming, &c.

He wrote on Titles and Entails:
But little here his toil avails;
For bit by bit the fabric fails,
    And nearly smothers Lothian.

    But why sae very lang o' coming? &c.

In Teinds or Tithes he deep did search:
But these, too, left him in the lurch;
The Liberals cashiered the Church,
    Just out of spite to Lothian.

    But what made him sae lang o' coming? &c.

Yet still he worked 'gainst wind and weather,
Till Brougham one morning broke his tether,
Abolished Scotch Law altogether,
   And fairly finished Lothian.

*   But why was he sae lang o' coming?*
*   Why sae very lang o' coming?*
*   Surely he was lang o' coming;*
*   So good-night to Lothian!*

THE JOLLY TESTATOR WHO MAKES HIS OWN WILL.

AIR—*Argyll is my name.*

YE Lawyers who live upon litigants' fees,
   And who need a good many to live at your ease;
Grave or gay, wise or witty, whate'er your degree,
Plain stuff or Queen's Counsel, take counsel of me.
When a festive occasion your spirit unbends,
You should never forget the Profession's best friends;
So we'll send round the wine and a bright bumper fill
To the jolly Testator who makes his own Will.

He premises his wish and his purpose to save
All disputes among friends when he's laid in his grave;
Then he straightway proceeds more disputes to create
Than a long summer's day would give time to relate.
He writes and erases, he blunders and blots,
He produces such puzzles and Gordian knots,
That a lawyer, intending to frame the deed *ill*,
Couldn't match the Testator who makes his own Will.

Testators are good; but a feeling more tender
Springs up when I think of the feminine gender:
The Testatrix for me, who, like Telemaque's mother,
Unweaves at one time what she wove at another.
She bequeaths, she repeats, she recalls a donation,
And she ends by revoking her own revocation;
Still scribbling or scratching some new Codicil;
O! success to the Woman who makes her own Will.

'Tisn't easy to say, 'mid her varying vapours,
What scraps should be deemed Testamentary papers;
'Tisn't easy from these her intentions to find,
When, perhaps, she herself never knew her own mind.
Every step that we take, there arises fresh trouble:
Is the legacy lapsed? is it single or double?
No customer brings so much grist to the mill
As the wealthy old Woman who makes her own Will.

The Law decides questions of *meum* and *tuum*,
By kindly consenting to make the thing *suum:*
The Esopean fable instructively tells
What becomes of the oyster, and who get the shells.
The Legatees starve, but the Lawyers are fed;
The Seniors have riches, the Juniors have bread;
The available surplus, of course, will be Nil
From the worthy Testators who make their own Will.

You had better pay toll when you take to the road,
Than attempt by a byway to reach your abode;
You had better employ a Conveyancer's hand,
Than encounter the risk that your Will shouldn't stand.
From the broad beaten track when the traveller strays,
He may land in a bog, or be lost in a maze;
And the Law, when defied, will revenge itself still
On the Man and the Woman who make their own Will.

HEY FOR SOCIAL SCIENCE, O!

A SONG FOR THE SOCIAL SCIENCE MEETING
AT GLASGOW IN 1860.

AIR—*Green grow the rashes, O!*

A PLEASANT week I lately passed
   In Glasgow town,—no, city, O!
With men of state and merchants great,
   And sages wise or witty O!

CHORUS—*Hey for Social Science, O!*
         Hey for Social Science, O!
         When wisdom, wine, and wit combine,
         They make a good alliance, O!

We met to show that all below
   To ruin fast is tending, O!
That laws and schools and prison rules
   Are much in need of mending, O!

    Hey for Social Science, &c.

But though, no doubt, 'twas well made out
    That things are old and wheezy, O!
O cursed spite! to set them right
    Was not so very easy, O!
      Hey for Social Science, &c.

Yet though the task may patience ask,
    We're here convened to try it, O!
To see if schools will root out fools,
    Or crime be cured by diet, O!
      Hey for Social Science, &c.

The blood-red sun had scarce begun
    To shine out strong and hearty, O!
When up we rose and donned our clo'es
    To join Bell's breakfast-party, O!
      Hey for Social Science, &c.

Delicious doles of meat and rolls
    Disposed to mirth and laughter, O!
The inspiring tea brought out Macnee,
    And others followed after, O!
      Hey for Social Science, &c.

When hunger's rage we thus assuage,
    Succeeds the thirst for knowledge, O!

Then, horse and foot, we take the *route*,
   And hurry to the College, O!

    Hey for Social Science, &c.

Here in we press for some Address
   That lasts two hours or longer, O!
And if a word is seldom heard,
   The applause is all the stronger, O!

    Hey for Social Science, &c.

The Section meetings next we try,
   Some worse and others better, O!
But if the days are somewhat dry,
   The nights will prove the wetter, O!

    Hey for Social Science, &c.

That sense alone conspicuous shone
   I can't declare in conscience, O!
But great's the use to introduce
   A safety-valve for nonsense, O!

    Hey for Social Science, &c.

A few who well their tale could tell
   Did ably fill the rostrums, O!

While many a goose his clack let loose,
   And quacks proclaimed their nostrums, O!
      Hey for Social Science, &c.

Just ere the welcome hour of six
   We gladly cut our cable, O!
And in some port of refuge fix,
   Hard by a well-spread table, O!
      Hey for Social Science, &c.

While all things good in drink and food
   Our weary souls are cheering, O!
The ills of life, before so rife,
   Seem quickly disappearing, O!
      Hey for Social Science, &c.

Around us eyes and faces bright
   Our softened hearts are winning, O!
Fair matrons in meridian light,
   And morning stars beginning, O!

> *Hey for Social Science, O!*
>   *The best of Social Science, O!*
> *Is when its power, in hall or bower,*
>   *To Beauty we affiance, O!*

With ardour fired, by love inspired,
   I rise and give "The Ladies," O!
And they who shrink the toast to drink
   May hang, and go to Hades, O!

    Hey for Social Science, &c.

We talk, we quaff, we sing and laugh,
   Then part with tears and sighing, O!
And when at last the week is past
   We're dead with mirth—or dying, O!

    Hey for Social Science, &c.

But I ordain that soon again,
   These pleasant hours repeating, O!
We learn some more of Social lore
   At such an evening meeting, O!

    Hey for Social Science, O!
      For genuine Social Science, O!
    A summons here to recompear
      Would find a quick compliance, O!

THE SHERIFF'S LIFE AT SEA:

BEING PASSAGES IN THE LIFE OF A MARITIME SHERIFF.

AIR—*The Sailor's Life at Sea.*

HOW gay is the Sheriff's roving life,
   Who from East to West can roam, boys:
How pleasant, with, or without, his wife,
   To sail for his Island home, boys. (*bis*)
      Roaming here,
      Foaming there,
      Merrily, cheerily,
      Readily, steadily;
Many an hour of mirth and glee
Has the Sheriff's life at sea, my boys.

When the steam is up and the goods are stored,
   And 'tis time to leave the Forth, boys,
The Sheriff gaily steps on board
   And steers away for the North, boys. (*bis*)

Steering here,
Veering there,
Merrily, cheerily,
Readily, steadily;
Quite from care and business free
Is the Sheriff's life at sea, my boys.

But the vessel breasts the eastern breeze,
And St Andrews Bay is near, boys;
And the Sheriff tries to look at his ease,
Though he feels a little queer, boys. (*bis*)
Pitching here,
Twitching there,
Cheerily, wearily,
Ruefully, woefully;
Much inclined to make Dundee
Is the Sheriff now at sea, my boys.

Then the vessel nears to Aberdeen,
And the plot is growing thick, boys:
On dinner bent the rest are seen,
But the Sheriff's fairly sick, boys. (*bis*)
Cooking here,
Puking there,
Drearily, wearily,
Groaningly, moaningly;

Plain it is he don't agree
With a Sheriff's life at sea, my boys.

Yet afloat once more, when the waves are calm,
  He tempts the treacherous main, boys;
And the Sheriff cures the coming qualm
  With a glass of good champagne, boys. (*bis*)
      Quaffing here,
      Laughing there,
      Cheerily, merrily,
      Readily, steadily;
Quite intent upon a spree,
Is the Sheriff now at sea, my boys.

But the zephyr soon becomes a gale,
  And the straining vessel groans, boys;
And the Sheriff's face grows deadly pale,
  As he thinks of Davy Jones, boys. (*bis*)
      Thinking here,
      Sinking there,
      Wearily, drearily,
      Shakingly, quakingly;
Not from fear or sickness free
Is the Sheriff now at sea, my boys.

So the Sheriff here must needs resign,
  For his inside's fairly gone, boys:

And he calls for a glass of brandy-wine,
   And to bed with his gaiters on, boys. (*bis*)
      Lying here,
      Dying there,
      Drearily, wearily,
      Groaningly, moaningly;
Prostrate laid by fate's decree
Seems the Sheriff now at sea, my boys.

But a joyful strain awakes the Muse,
   Which will quite efface the past, boys;
For the Mail-boat brings the joyful news
   That promotion's come at last, boys. (*bis*)
      Cheering here,
      Jeering there,
      Merrily, cheerily,
      Readily, steadily;
Fear and sickness far may flee,
For the Sheriff quits the sea, my boys.

NOTE.—This song, describing the imaginary voyage of a Scotch Sheriff to his maritime dominions, was written as a parody on the song of "The Sailor's Life at Sea," which was one of the lyrics so delightfully sung by Professor Wilson. Another parody, in a different style, and by a different but certainly not an inferior hand, appeared in the Magazine under the title of "The Bagman's Life on Shore," May 1838.

L'Envoy.

I SEE how other men aspire,
   Who lofty strains can nobly raise;
And feel that this, my humble lyre,
   Must yield to them the meed of praise.

But Mirth may come to Virtue's aid,
   When gloom the face of heaven would hide;
And Truth, in mirthful garb arrayed,
   Finds entrance that were else denied.

Then scorn not thou the sportive lay,
   Nor judge it by the rigid letter;
By smiling paths it winds its way,
   With covert aim, to make men better.

MUSIC

OF SOME OF THE PRECEDING SONGS.

Original or Adapted.

A FLASK OF ROSY WINE.

To make life's pul - ses gai - ly go, Not much too fast, nor

yet too slow; And joy with - out de - jec - tion know, Were

worth a gold - en mine. Then try with me the sim - ple

art, If bet - ter views you can't im - part, To calm the

brain and cheer the heart, With a flask of ros - y Wine.

I'M VERY FOND OF WATER.

I'm ve-ry fond of wa-ter, I drink it noon and night; Not Re-chab's son or daugh-ter Had there-in more de-light. I break-fast on it dai-ly; And nec-tar it doth seem, When once I've mix'd it gai-ly With su-gar and with cream. But I for-got to men-tion That in it first I see, In-fused or in sus-pen-sion, Good Mo-cha or Bo-hea.

THE PERMISSIVE BILL.

"Pray, what is this Per-mis-sive Bill, That some folks

rave a-bout? I can't, with all my pains and skill, Its

mean-ing quite make out." O! it's a lit-tle

sim-ple Bill, That seeks to pass *in-cog.*, To *per-*

mit ME to *pre-vent* you from hav-ing a glass of grog.

A BOTTLE AND FRIEND.

When the even-ing of life comes with tem-per-ate ray To

cool the hot blood that has boil'd all the day; When our

fac-ul-ties flag, and our fro-lics are o'er, And our

fav-our-ite i-dols are wor-shipp'd no more; May some so-ber

plea-sures that sea-son at-tend, And Fortune still leave us — a

Bot-tle and Friend, A Bot-tle and Friend, A Bot-tle and

Friend, And For-tune still leave us — a Bot-tle and Friend.

THE SHERIFF'S LIFE AT SEA.

PRINTED BY WILLIAM BLACKWOOD AND SONS, EDINBURGH.

MESSRS BLACKWOOD AND SONS'

RECENT PUBLICATIONS.

—o—

Lays of the Scottish Cavaliers,
And other Poems. By W. EDMONDSTOUNE AYTOUN, D.C.L., Professor of Rhetoric and English Literature in the University of Edinburgh. Nineteenth Edition. Fcap. 8vo, 7s. 6d.

"Professor Aytoun's 'Lays of the Scottish Cavaliers'—a volume of verse which shows that Scotland has yet a poet. Full of the true fire, it now stirs and swells like a trumpet-note—now sinks in cadences sad and wild as the wail of a Highland dirge."—*Quarterly Review.*

Illustrated Edition of the
Lays of the Scottish Cavaliers.
The Designs by Sir J. NOEL PATON, R.S.A. Engraved on Wood by John Thompson, W. J. Linton, W. Thomas, J. W. Whymper, J. Cooper, W. T. Green, Dalziel Brothers, E. Evans, J. Adam, &c. Small 4to, printed on toned paper, bound in gilt cloth, 21s.

"The artists have excelled themselves in the engravings which they have furnished. Seizing the spirit of Mr Aytoun's 'Ballads' as perhaps none but Scotchmen could have seized it, they have thrown their whole strength into the work with a heartiness which others would do well to imitate. Whoever there may be that does not already know these 'Lays,' we recommend at once to make their acquaintance in this edition, wherein author and artist illustrate each other as kindred spirits should."—*Standard.*

Bothwell: A Poem.
By W. EDMONDSTOUNE AYTOUN, DC.L. Third Edition. Fcap. 8vo, 7s. 6d.

"Professor Aytoun has produced a fine poem and an able argument, and 'Bothwell' will assuredly take its stand among the classics of Scottish literature."—*The Press.*

The Ballads of Scotland.
Edited by Professor AYTOUN. Second Edition. 2 vols. fcap. 8vo, 12s.

"No country can boast of a richer collection of Ballads than Scotland, and no Editor for these Ballads could be found more accomplished than Professor Aytoun. He has sent forth two beautiful volumes which range with 'Percy's Reliques'—which, for completeness and accuracy, leave little to be desired—which must henceforth be considered as the standard edition of the Scottish Ballads, and which we commend as a model to any among ourselves who may think of doing like service to the English Ballads."—*Times*.

Poems and Ballads of Goethe.
Translated by Professor AYTOUN and THEODORE MARTIN. Second Edition. Fcap. 8vo, 6s.

"There is no doubt that these are the best translations of Goethe's marvellously-cut gems which have yet been published."—*Times*.

Faust: A Dramatic Poem.
By GOETHE. Translated into English Verse by THEODORE MARTIN. In 1 vol. post 8vo, 6s.

The Book of Ballads.
Edited by BON GAULTIER. Ninth Edition, with numerous Illustrations by DOYLE, LEECH, and CROWQUILL. Gilt edges, post 8vo, 8s. 6d.

Firmilian; or, the Student of Badajos.
A Spasmodic Tragedy. By T. PERCY JONES. In small 8vo, 5s.

"Humour of a kind most rare at all times, and especially in the present day, runs through every page, and passages of true poetry and delicious versification prevent the continual play of sarcasm from becoming tedious."—*Literary Gazette*.

The Odyssey of Homer.
Translated into English Verse in the Spenserian Stanza. By PHILIP STANHOPE WORSLEY, M.A., Scholar of Corpus Christi College. 2 vols. crown 8vo, 18s.

"Mr Worsley,—applying the Spenserian stanza, that beautiful romantic measure, to the most romantic poem of the ancient world—making the stanza yield him, too (what it never yielded to Byron), its treasures of fluidity and sweet ease—above all, bringing to his task a truly poetical sense and skill,—has produced a version of the 'Odyssey' much the most pleasing of those hitherto produced, and which is delightful to read."—*Professor Arnold on Translating Homer*.

The Iliad of Homer.
Translated into English Verse in the Spenserian Stanza. Books I. to XII. By PHILIP S. WORSLEY, M.A. Books XIII. to XXIV. By Professor CONINGTON, Oxford.
2 vols. crown 8vo, 21s.

Poems and Translations.
>By PHILIP STANHOPE WORSLEY, M.A., Scholar of Corpus Christi College, Oxford. Fcap. 8vo, 5s.

The Poems of Felicia Hemans.
>Complete in 1 vol. royal 8vo, with Portrait by FINDEN. Cheap Edition, 12s. 6d. *Another Edition*, with Memoir by her SISTER. Seven vols. fcap., 35s. *Another Edition*, in 6 vols. bound in 3, cloth, 12s. 6d.
>
>The following Works of Mrs HEMANS are sold separately, bound in cloth, gilt edges, 4s. each :—
>
>RECORDS OF WOMAN. FOREST SANCTUARY. SONGS OF THE AFFECTIONS. DRAMATIC WORKS. TALES AND HISTORIC SCENES. MORAL AND RELIGIOUS POEMS.

Selections from the Poems of Mrs Hemans.
>Beautifully printed on toned paper, bound in gilt cloth, 5s.

Uniform with the above.

The Poetical Works of Caroline Bowles Southey.
>Collected Edition. Small fcap., cloth, gilt edges, 5s.

Uniform with the above.

The Course of Time: A Poem.
>By ROBERT POLLOK, A.M. Twenty-fifth Edition. With Memoir. Small fcap. 8vo, cloth, gilt edges, 3s. 6d.
>
>"Of deep and hallowed impress, full of noble thoughts and graphic conceptions—the production of a mind alive to the great relations of being, and the sublime simplicity of our religion."—*Blackwood's Magazine.*

Poetical Works of Thomas Aird.
>Fourth Edition. In 1 vol. fcap. 8vo, 6s.

Poems.
>By the Lady FLORA HASTINGS. Edited by her SISTER. Second Edition, with a Portrait. Fcap., 7s. 6d.

Poetical Works of D. M. Moir.
With Portrait, and Memoir by THOMAS AIRD. Second Edition. 2 vols. fcap. 8vo, 12s.

Lectures on the Poetical Literature of the Past Half-Century.
By D. M. MOIR (Δ). Second Edition. Fcap. 8vo, 5s.

"A delightful volume."—*Morning Chronicle.*
"Exquisite in its taste and generous in its criticisms."—*Hugh Miller.*

An Illustrated Edition of the Course of Time.
In large 8vo, bound in cloth, richly gilt, 21s.

"There has been no modern poem in the English language, of the class to which the 'Course of Time' belongs, since Milton wrote, that can be compared to it. In the present instance the artistic talents of Messrs FOSTER, CLAYTON, TENNIEL, EVANS, DALZIEL, GREEN, and WOODS, have been employed in giving expression to the sublimity of the language, by equally exquisite illustrations, all of which are of the highest class."—*Bell's Messenger.*

Poems and Ballads of Schiller.
Translated by Lord LYTTON. Second Edition. 8vo, 10s. 6d.

Sir William Crichton—Athelwold—Guidone:
Dramas by WILLIAM SMITH, Author of 'Thorndale,' &c. 32mo, 2s. 6d.

Illustrations of the Lyric Poetry and Music of Scotland.
By WILLIAM STENHOUSE. Originally compiled to accompany the 'Scots Musical Museum,' and now published separately, with Additional Notes and Illustrations. 8vo, 7s. 6d.

Professor Wilson's Poems.
Containing the 'Isle of Palms,' the 'City of the Plague,' 'Unimore,' and other Poems. Complete Edition. Crown 8vo, 4s.

Poems and Songs.
By DAVID WINGATE. Second Edition. Fcap. 8vo, 5s.

"We are delighted to welcome into the brotherhood of real poets a countryman of Burns, and whose verse will go far to render the rougher Border Scotch a classic dialect in our literature."—*John Bull.*

Lady Lee's Widowhood.
  By Lieut.-Col. E. B. HAMLEY. Crown 8vo, with 13 Illustrations by the Author. 6s.

The Odes of Horace.
  With Life and Notes. Translated by THEODORE MARTIN. Second Edition. Post 8vo, 9s.

Catullus.
  With Life and Notes. Translated by the same. Post 8vo, 6s. 6d.

The Vita Nuova of Dante.
  With an Introduction and Notes. Translated by the same. Square 8vo, 7s. 6d.

Aladdin: A Dramatic Poem.
  By ADAM OEHLENSCHLAEGER. Translated by the same. Fcap. 8vo, 5s.

Correggio: A Tragedy.
  By OEHLENSCHLAEGER. Translated by the same. With Notes. Fcap. 8vo, 3s.

King Rene's Daughter: A Danish Lyrical Drama.
  By HENRIK HERTZ. Translated by the same. Second Edition. Fcap., 2s. 6d.

Thorndale; or, the Conflict of Opinion.
  By WILLIAM SMITH. Second Edition. Crown 8vo, 10s. 6d.

Gravenhurst; or, Thoughts on Good and Evil.
  By WILLIAM SMITH, Author of 'Thorndale,' &c. In crown 8vo, price 7s. 6d.

  "One of those rare books which, being filled with noble and beautiful thoughts, deserves an attentive and thoughtful perusal." – *Westminster Review.*

Lord Lytton's Novels.

Library Edition. Printed from a large and readable type. In Volumes of a convenient and handsome form. 8vo, 5s. each—viz. :

THE CAXTON NOVELS, 10 Volumes :

The Caxton Family. 2 vols.	What will he do with it? 4 vols.
My Novel. 4 vols.	

HISTORICAL ROMANCES, 11 Volumes :

Devereux. 2 vols.	The Siege of Grenada. 1 vol.
The Last Days of Pompeii. 2 vols.	The Last of the Barons. 2 vols.
Rienzi. 2 vols.	Harold. 2 vols.

ROMANCES, 7 Volumes :

The Pilgrims of the Rhine. 1 vol.	Zanoni. 2 vols.
Eugene Aram. 2 vols.	A Strange Story. 2 vols.

NOVELS OF LIFE AND MANNERS, 15 Volumes :

Pelham. 2 vols.	Ernest Maltravers—Second Part (*i.e.* Alice). 2 vols.
The Disowned. 2 vols.	
Paul Clifford. 2 vols.	
Godolphin. 1 vol.	Night and Morning. 2 vols.
Ernest Maltravers—First Part. 2 vols.	Lucretia. 2 vols.

"It is of the handiest of sizes; the paper is good; and the type, which seems to be new, is very clear and beautiful. There are no pictures. The whole charm of the presentment of the volume consists in its handiness, and the tempting clearness and beauty of the type, which almost converts into a pleasure the mere act of following the printer's lines, and leaves the author's mind free to exert its unobstructed force upon the reader."—*Examiner.*

"Nothing could be better as to size, type, paper, and general get-up."—*Athenæum.*

The Novels of George Eliot.

Cheap Edition, 4 vols. crown 8vo—viz. :

ADAM BEDE. With 7 Illustrations. 3s. 6d.
THE MILL ON THE FLOSS. With 7 Illustrations. 3s. 6d.
SILAS MARNER. With Illustrations.
SCENES OF CLERICAL LIFE. With Illustrations.

Felix Holt, the Radical.
By GEORGE ELIOT, Author of 'Adam Bede,' &c.

"Upon the midlands now the industrious muse doth fall,
The shires which we the heart of England well may call.
  .   .   .   .
My native country thou, which so brave spirits hast bred,
If there be virtues yet remaining in thy earth,
Or any good of thine thou bred'st into my birth,
Accept it as thine own, whilst now I sing of thee,
Of all thy later brood the unworthiest though I be."
—DRAYTON'S *Polyolbion*.

In 2 vols. crown 8vo, cloth gilt, 12s.

Katie Stewart: A True Story.
By Mrs OLIPHANT. Fcap. 8vo, with Frontispiece and Vignette, 4s.

Tom Cringle's Log.
A New Edition. With Illustrations by STANFIELD, WEIR, SKELTON, WALKER, &c., Engraved by WHYMPER. Crown 8vo, 6s.

"Everybody who has failed to read 'Tom Cringle's Log' should do so at once. The Quarterly Review' went so far as to say that the papers composing it, when it first appeared in 'Blackwood,' were the most brilliant series of the time, and that time one unrivalled for the number of famous magazinists existing in it. Coleridge says, in his 'Table Talk,' that the 'Log' is most excellent; and these verdicts have been ratified by generations of men and boys, and by the manifestation of Continental approval which is shown by repeated translations. The engravings illustrating the present issue are excellent."—*Standard*.

Chapters on Churchyards.
By Mrs SOUTHEY. Fcap. 8vo, 7s. 6d.

Tony Butler.
Originally published in 'Blackwood's Magazine.' 3 vols. post 8vo, £1, 11s. 6d.

"No novel of the season has given us so much genuine pleasure; and we can with safety predict that every reader will be delighted with it. Skeff Damer, and Tony, and Count M'Caskey, will live in the memory for many a day. They are all three, in their way, perfectly original conceptions, and are as true to the life as any portraits ever drawn by pen and ink."—*Standard*.

Sir Brook Fossbrooke.
By CHARLES LEVER. Crown 8vo, 6s.

Chronicles of Carlingford:
Salem Chapel. Second Edition. Complete in 1 vol., price 5s.

"This story, so fresh, so powerfully written, and so tragic, stands out from among its fellows like a piece of newly-coined gold in a handful of dim commonplace shillings. Tales of pastoral experience and scenes from clerical life we have had in plenty, but the sacred things of the conventicle, the relative position of pastor and flock in a Nonconforming 'connection,' were but guessed at by the world outside, and terrible is the revelation."—*Westminster Review.*

The Rector, and The Doctor's Family. Post 8vo, 4s.

The Perpetual Curate. 6s.

"We can only repeat the expression of our admiration for a work which bears on every page the evidence of close observation and the keenest insight, united to real dramatic feeling and a style of unusual eloquence and power."—*Westminster Review.*

"The 'Perpetual Curate' is nevertheless one of the best pictures of Clerical Life that has ever been drawn, and it is essentially true."—*Times.*

Miss Marjoribanks. 6s.

Tales from Blackwood.
Complete in 12 vols., bound in cloth, 18s. The Volumes are sold separately, 1s. 6d.; and may be had of most Booksellers, in Six Volumes, handsomely half-bound in red morocco.

CONTENTS.

VOL. I. The Glenmutchkin Railway.—Vanderdecken's Message Home.—The Floating Beacon.—Colonna the Painter.—Napoleon.—A Legend of Gibraltar.—The Iron Shroud.

VOL. II. Lazaro's Legacy.—A Story without a Tail.—Faustus and Queen Elizabeth.—How I became a Yeoman.—Devereux Hall.—The Metempsychosis.—College Theatricals.

VOL. III. A Reading Party in the Long Vacation.—Father Tom and the Pope.—La Petite Madelaine.—Bob Burke's Duel with Ensign Brady.—The Headsman: A Tale of Doom.—The Wearyful Woman.

VOL. IV. How I stood for the Dreepdaily Burghs.—First and Last.—The Duke's Dilemma: A Chronicle of Niesenstein.—The Old Gentleman's Teetotum.—"Woe to us when we lose the Watery Wall."—My College Friends: Charles Russell, the Gentleman Commoner.—The Magic Lay of the One-Horse Chay.

Tales from Blackwood—continued.

- Vol. V. Adventures in Texas.—How we got Possession of the Tuileries.—Captain Paton's Lament.—The Village Doctor.—A Singular Letter from Southern Africa.

- Vol. VI. My Friend the Dutchman.—My College Friends—No. II.: Horace Leicester.—The Emerald Studs.—My College Friends—No. III.: Mr W. Wellington Hurst.—Christine: A Dutch Story.—The Man in the Bell.

- Vol. VII. My English Acquaintance.—The Murderer's Last Night.—Narration of Certain Uncommon Things that did formerly happen to Me, Herbert Willis, B.D.—The Wags.—The Wet Wooing: A Narrative of '98.—Ben-na-Groich.

- Vol. VIII. The Surveyor's Tale.—The Forrest-Race Romance.—Di Vasari: A Tale of Florence.—Sigismund Fatello.—The Boxes.

- Vol. IX. Rosaura: A Tale of Madrid.—Adventure in the North-West Territory.—Harry Bolton's Curacy.—The Florida Pirate.—The Pandour and his Princess.—The Beauty Draught.

- Vol. X. Antonio di Carara.—The Fatal Repast.—The Vision of Cagliostro.—The First and Last Kiss.—The Smuggler's Leap.—The Haunted and the Haunters.—The Duellists.

- Vol. XI. The Natolian Story-Teller.—The First and Last Crime.—John Rintoul.—Major Moss.—The Premier and his Wife.

- Vol. XII. Tickler among the Thieves!—The Bridegroom of Barna.—The Involuntary Experimentalist.—Lebrun's Lawsuit.—The Snowing-up of Strath Lugas.—A Few Words on Social Philosophy.

Lights and Shadows of Scottish Life.
Fcap. 8vo, 3s. cloth.

The Life of Mansie Wauch,
Tailor in Dalkeith. Fcap. 8vo, 3s. cloth.

The Subaltern.
By the Author of 'The Chelsea Pensioners.' Fcap. 8vo, 3s. cloth.

Peninsular Scenes and Sketches.
By the Author of 'The Student of Salamanca.' Fcap. 8vo, 3s. cloth.

Nights at Mess, Sir Frizzle Pumpkin, and other Tales. Fcap. 8vo, 3s. cloth.

The Youth and Manhood of Cyril Thornton.
By the Author of 'Men and Manners in America.' Fcap. 8vo, 4s. cloth.

Valerius: A Roman Story.
Fcap. 8vo, 3s. cloth.

Reginald Dalton.
By the Author of 'Valerius.' Fcap. 8vo, 4s. cloth.

Some Passages in the Life of Adam Blair, and History of Matthew Wald. By the Author of 'Valerius.' Fcap. 8vo, 4s. cloth.

Annals of the Parish, and Ayrshire Legatees.
By JOHN GALT. Fcap. 8vo, 4s. cloth.

Sir Andrew Wylie.
By JOHN GALT. Fcap. 8vo, 4s. cloth.

The Provost, and other Tales.
By JOHN GALT. Fcap. 8vo, 4s. cloth.

The Entail.
By JOHN GALT. Fcap. 8vo, 4s. cloth.

Recent Publications.

The Wonder-Seeker;
Or, The History of Charles Douglas. By M. FRASER TYTLER, Author of 'Tales of the Great and Brave,' &c. A New Edition. Fcap. 8vo, 3s. 6d.

The Diary of a Late Physician.
By SAMUEL WARREN, D.C.L. 1 vol. crown 8vo, 5s. 6d.

Ten Thousand a-Year.
By SAMUEL WARREN, D.C.L. 2 vols. crown 8vo, 9s.

Now and Then.
By SAMUEL WARREN, D.C.L. Crown 8vo, 2s. 6d.

Recreations of Christopher North.
By Professor WILSON. In 2 vols. crown 8vo, 8s.

The Noctes Ambrosianæ.
By Professor WILSON. With Notes and a Glossary. In 4 vols. crown 8vo, 16s.

Tales.
By Professor WILSON. Comprising 'The Lights and Shadows of Scottish Life,' 'The Trials of Margaret Lyndsay,' and 'The Foresters.' In 1 vol. crown 8vo, 4s. cloth.

The Book-Hunter, etc.
By JOHN HILL BURTON. New Edition. In crown 8vo, 7s. 6d.

" A book pleasant to look at and pleasant to read—pleasant from its rich store of anecdote, its geniality, and its humour, even to persons who care little for the subjects of which it treats, but beyond measure delightful to those who are in any degree members of the above-mentioned fraternity."—*Saturday Review.*

" We have not been more amused for a long time; and every reader who takes interest in typography and its consequences will say the same, if he will begin to read; beginning, he will finish, and be sorry when it is over."—*Athenæum.*

" Mr Burton has now given us a pleasant book, full of quaint anecdote, and of a lively bookish talk. There is a quiet humour in it which is very taking, and there is a curious knowledge of books which is really very sound."—*Examiner.*

The Cairngorm Mountains.

By JOHN HILL BURTON. In crown 8vo, 3s. 6d.

"One of the most complete as well as most lively and intelligent bits of reading that the lover of works of travel has seen for many a day."—*Saturday Review*.

The Scot Abroad,

And the Ancient League with France. By JOHN HILL BURTON, Author of 'The Book-Hunter, etc.' 2 vols. crown 8vo, in Roxburghe binding, 15s.

"Mr Burton's lively and interesting 'Scot Abroad,' not the least valuable of his contributions to the historical literature of his country."—*Quarterly Review*.

"An excellent book, that will interest Englishmen and fascinate Scotchmen."—*Times*.

"No amount of selections, detached at random, can give an adequate idea of the varied and copious results of reading which are stored up in the compact and pithy pages of 'The Scot Abroad.'"—*Saturday Review*.

"A charming book."—*Spectator*.

Lives of the Queens of Scotland,

And English Princesses connected with the Regal Succession of Great Britain. By AGNES STRICKLAND. With Portraits and Historical Vignettes. Post 8vo, £4, 4s.

Memorials of the Castle of Edinburgh.

By JAMES GRANT. A New Edition. In crown 8vo, with 12 Engravings, 3s. 6d.

The Great Governing Families of England.

By J. LANGTON SANFORD and MEREDITH TOWNSEND. *Contents:*—The Percies—The Greys of Howick—The Lowthers—The Vanes or Fanes—the Stanleys of Knowsley—The Grosvenors—The Fitzwilliams—The Cavendishes—The Bentincks—The Clintons—The Stanhopes—The Talbots—The Leveson-Gowers—The Pagets—The Manners—The Montagus—The Osbornes—The Fitzroys—The Spencers—The Grenvilles—The Russells—The Cecils—The Villiers—The Barings—The Petty-Fitzmaurices—The Herberts—The Somersets—The Berkeleys—The Seymours—The Lennoxes—The Howards.

2 vols. 8vo, £1, 8s. in extra binding, with richly gilt cover.

Homer and his Translators,
And the Greek Drama. By Professor WILSON. Crown 8vo, 6s.

"But of all the criticisms on Homer which I have ever had the good fortune to read, in our own or any language, the most vivid and entirely genial are those found in the 'Essays, Critical and Imaginative,' of the late Professor Wilson."—*Mr Gladstone's Studies on Homer.*

The Sketcher.
By the Rev. JOHN EAGLES. Originally published in 'Blackwood's Magazine.' 8vo, 10s. 6d.

"This volume, called by the appropriate name of 'The Sketcher,' is one that ought to be found in the studio of every English landscape-painter. . . . More instructive and suggestive readings for young artists, especially landscape-painters, can scarcely be found."—*The Globe.*

Caxtoniana:
A Series of Essays on LIFE, LITERATURE, and MANNERS. By Lord LYTTON. 2 vols. crown 8vo, 21s.

"It would be very possible to fill many pages with the wise bright things of these volumes."—*Eclectic.*

"Gems of thought, set upon some of the most important subjects that can engage the attention of men."—*Daily News.*

Essays on Social Subjects.
From the 'Saturday Review.' Crown 8vo, 7s. 6d. Third Edition. A Second Series of the same, 7s. 6d.

"In their own way of simple, straightforward reflection upon life, the present century has produced no essays better than these."—*Examiner.*

"We shall welcome the author again if he has more to say on topics which he treats so well."—*Guardian.*

Lectures on the History of Literature,
Ancient and Modern. From the German of F. SCHLEGEL. Fcap., 5s.

"A wonderful performance—better than anything we as yet have in our own language."—*Quarterly Review.*

Geology for General Readers.
A Series of Popular Sketches in Geology and Palæontology. By DAVID PAGE, LL.D. F.R.S.E. F.G.S. Second Edition, containing several new Chapters, price 6s.

Religion in Common Life:

A Sermon preached in Crathie Church, October 14, 1855, before Her Majesty the Queen and Prince Albert. By the Rev. JOHN CAIRD, D.D. Published by Her Majesty's Command. Bound in cloth, 8d. Cheap Edition, 3d.

Sermons.

By the Rev. JOHN CAIRD, D.D., Professor of Divinity in the University of Glasgow, and one of Her Majesty's Chaplains for Scotland. In crown 8vo, 5s. This Edition includes the Sermon on 'Religion in Common Life,' preached in Crathie Church, Oct. 1855, before Her Majesty the Queen and the late Prince Consort.

"They are noble sermons; and we are not sure but that, with the cultivated reader, they will gain rather than lose by being read, not heard. There is a thoughtfulness and depth about them which can hardly be appreciated, unless when they are studied at leisure; and there are so many sentences so felicitously expressed that we should grudge being hurried away from them by a rapid speaker, without being allowed to enjoy them a second time."—*Fraser's Magazine.*

The Mother's Legacie to her Unborne Childe.

By Mrs ELIZABETH JOCELINE. Edited by the Very Rev. Principal LEE. 32mo, 4s. 6d.

"This beautiful and touching legacie."—*Athenæum.*
"A delightful monument of the piety and high feeling of a truly noble mother."—*Morning Advertiser.*

Family Prayers,

As authorised by the General Assembly of the Church of Scotland, with other Prayers by the Committee of the General Assembly on Aids to Devotion, forming a Course of Prayers for Four Weeks. Crown 8vo, red edges, price 4s. 6d.

The Christian Life,

In its Origin, Progress, and Perfection. By the Very Rev. E. B. RAMSAY, LL.D. F.R.S.E., Dean of the Diocese of Edinburgh. Crown 8vo, 9s.

Memoir of Professor Aytoun.
By THEODORE MARTIN. Post 8vo, cloth, with Portrait on steel, 12s.

The Life of St Columba, the Apostle of Caledonia.
Extracted from 'The Monks of the West,' by the COUNT DE MONTALEMBERT. Fcap. 8vo, 3s. 6d.

Spindrift.
By Sir JOSEPH NOEL PATON. Fcap. 8vo, 5s.
"Mere spindrift, by the gusts of fancy blown."

Blackwood's Standard Novels.
TOM CRINGLE'S LOG. Fcap., boards, 2s.
CRUISE OF THE MIDGE. Fcap., boards, 2s.
CYRIL THORNTON. Fcap., boards, 2s.
MANSIE WAUCH. Fcap., paper cover, 1s.
SIR FRIZZLE PUMPKIN. Fcap., paper cover, 1s.
PENINSULAR SCENES AND SKETCHES. Fcap., paper cover, 1s.

Natural Theology:
An Inquiry into the Fundamental Principles of Religious, Moral, and Political Science. By W. R. PIRIE, D.D., Professor of Divinity and Church History in the University of Aberdeen. Fcap. 8vo, 5s.

The Increase of Faith.
Contents: — 1. Of the Nature of Faith. 2. Of the Aspirations of the Believer for Increase of Faith. 3. That Faith is capable of Increase. 4. Of Faith's Increase: What it is. 5. Of Faith as the Gift of God. 6. Of the Means of Faith's Increase. 7. Of the Hindrances to Faith's Increase. 8. Of the Assurance of Grace and Salvation. 9. Of Faith made Perfect. Fcap. 8vo, cloth, 3s. 6d.

DEDICATED BY PERMISSION TO
HIS ROYAL HIGHNESS THE PRINCE OF WALES.

THE

HANDY ROYAL ATLAS.

By ALEX. KEITH JOHNSTON,
LL.D. F.R.S.E. F.R.G.S. &c.

Author of the 'Royal Atlas,' the 'Physical Atlas,' &c.

This work has been constructed for the purpose of placing in the hands of the public a useful and thoroughly accurate ATLAS of Maps of Modern Geography, in a convenient form, and at a moderate price. It is based on the **'Royal Atlas,'** by the same Author; and, in so far as the scale permits, it comprises many of the excellences which its prototype is acknowledged to possess. The aim has been to make the book strictly what its name implies, a **Handy Atlas**—a valuable substitute for the 'Royal,' where that is too bulky or too expensive to find a place, a needful auxiliary to the junior branches of families, and a *vade mecum* to the tutor and the pupil-teacher.

45 MAPS, CLEARLY PRINTED AND CAREFULLY COLOURED, WITH GENERAL INDEX.

Imperial Quarto, price £2, 12s. 6d., half-bound morocco.

"The 'Handy Atlas' is thoroughly deserving of its name. Not only does it contain the latest information, but its size and arrangement render it perfect as a book of reference, and, in a scientific point of view, it will sustain a reputation so honourably acquired and so widely known as that of Mr Keith Johnston."—*Standard*.

W. BLACKWOOD & SONS, Edinburgh and London.

www.ingramcontent.com/pod-product-compliance
Lightning Source LLC
Chambersburg PA
CBHW030317170426
43202CB00009B/1044